ANOINTED

WITH

OIL

By: C. John Miller

As told to Jack R. Westbrook

Published by Jack R. Westbrook ORSB Publishing

POB 16, Mount Pleasant, Michigan 48804-0016

bluwndrer@aol.com

First Printing December, 2010

Printed by createspace.com

This book is dedicated to my wife, Reva, who kept home, hearth and four kids operating smoothly while I was off tilting at windmills, and who insisted that this book be written.

Also, a special dedication to the men and women who have in the past, and will in the future, devote their lives to outsmarting Mother Nature to find the petroleum treasures she's hidden beneath the earth to be discovered to fuel our way of life.

Anointed

With

Oil

My journey with faith from the oilfields of Michigan…
to the legislative halls of Washington, D.C., and back again.

By: C. John Miller

As told to Jack R. Westbrook

INTRODUCTION

The cornerstone of our 76-year old organization of Michigan oil and natural gas producers is the effectiveness of our elected chief executive. As was said of C. John Miller when he was first elected MOGA President in 1966, "…. he brings…an enthusiasm and confidence the industry needs, and which the Association has provided for many years." John received a standing acclamation from the MOGA Board of Directors in recognition of the service he had rendered in his first ten months in office. Demonstrating their continued confidence in him he was re-elected as President in 1967.

In addition to serving as President of the Michigan Oil And Gas Association, John served as President of the National Stripper Well Association and the Independent Petroleum Association of America. There is no doubt that John has played a significant role in shaping policy in our industry and continues to contribute to our collective services and mutual prosperity.

On his "Recognition Night," April 22, 1976, MOGA proudly "paid tribute to an outstanding citizen for dedication to faith, courage to his family, character to his community, intelligence, imagination and perseverance in service to the oil and gas industry of America. His loyal and devoted service is acknowledged with deep appreciation."

Is John Miller an outstanding individual? Yes. He is a person that has handed out priceless gifts, such as encouragement and inspiration. He stimulates the mind. He helps tremendously in smoothing over the rough spots—with no thought of reward. He has always gone out of his way to be decent and helpful in contacts with association staff at the state and national level. I know he will continue to make a big difference in people's lives. I also know that John has prayed for the strength to carry on his good work for our industry and will continue to add to all that he has accomplished.

One of the biggest reasons for John's success is the cooperation and encouragement he receives from his wife Reva J. (Pickitt) Miller. I know this is true, because I have witnessed it many times over the years.

John has been a true friend and I want to make my appreciation of who he is a matter of record. My own work over the last forty years as Chief Staff Executive with MOGA, has benefited greatly from the example and counsel derived from his preeminence and experience. For that, John, I thank you.

Frank L. Mortl
President & CEO
Michigan Oil And Gas Association
Lansing, Michigan

INTRODUCTION BY BARRY RUSSELL

For most of the public, the American oil and natural gas industry is misunderstood, if not entirely invisible. They would be surprised to learn of the contributions and the character of the 15,000 smaller independent oil and natural gas companies — the so-called "wildcatters." These American companies don't own refineries or gasoline stations, but instead explore and produce the nation's domestic crude oil and natural gas supplies. Because independents live where they work, they are good stewards of the environment and active members of their churches and communities. The true character of the American oil and natural gas producer – the "wildcatter" – is defined by integrity, education, hard work, risk-taking … a commitment to family, community, the nation.

John Miller honestly exemplifies this spirit – not only in his own business and personal life, but also in his commitment to this important American industry. John was first elected president of the Independent Petroleum Association of America (IPAA), in 1973, the very first week of the Israeli-Arab conflict, which led to the Arab embargoes on oil shipments to the U.S. This led the late Senator "Scoop" Jackson (D-WA) to malign the American oil industry as well. John was the industry's loudest voice against Sen. Jackson and his campaign to vilify the industry. He told the story, to anyone who would listen from coast to coast, of the American oil and natural gas producer and how the industry's health directly correlated to the health of the economy and national security. More criticisms of the industry would ensue over his tenure – calls for new taxes, price controls, and repeals of industry incentives would be the focus of an unfriendly Congress. John would visit Washington to meet with leaders like President Ford and to testify before 19 congressional committees -- more than any other industry representative.

Without John's strong defense of this industry, America would be more dependent on foreign oil today. In 1975, the Energy Information Newsletter commented about John: "The entire industry owes Miller much. So does the American public, although it does not yet understand how much."

In 1975, John was inducted into the Chief Roughnecks Hall of Fame, one of the industry's most significant honors. I'm reminded of what was said of John that day: "Articulate without being flamboyant, sincere in his presentation of hard facts and figures, utterly devoid of a self-serving motive except to help the industry into which he was born, Miller has spent the past two years establishing a record of political action that is without equal in the annals of the oil patch." Now, more than three decades later, these words still ring true.

For those of us lucky enough to have worked with John and to call him friend, I would add inspirational leader. On behalf of the industry, thank you, John.

Barry Russell, President and CEO
Independent Petroleum Association of America, Washington, D.C.

TABLE OF CONTENTS

FOREWORD

I started this project as a memoir to share with my family so that future generations of this branch of the Millers will know what happened to their ancestors during that murky time referred to as *back-in-the-day*.

My *back-in-the-day* was a tumultuous period for domestic oil and gas exploration and development from the time the U.S. industry celebrated its centennial in 1959 up to its 150th birthday in 2009. The exploration and production industry is comprised of the folks who look and drill for oil and natural gas, bring it to the surface and put it in a truck, a ship, or a pipeline to transport it to market. For simplicity's sake, the exploration and production segment of the oil and gas industry will be what I mean when I say oil and gas business throughout this narrative.

The accepted birthday of the U.S. oil and gas business is August 29, 1859, when Col. Edwin Drake brought in the first commercially producing well in Titusville, Pennsylvania. In 1959, during its 100th anniversary, the oil and gas industry's history was lauded by the "three P's"—Politicians, Press and Public—as a shining symbol of American virtues. At that time, innumerable articles proclaimed the entrepreneurship, bravery, skill and heroism of those who took risks to drill into the earth against staggering odds to tap into the oil and natural gas needed to feed the voracious energy appetite of America's lifestyle, and our country celebrated our energy explorers with festive parades, with glittering speeches and with high adulation in the press and over the airways. Mind, too, that back then, we imported less than twenty percent of the crude oil we used domestically.

How different when a half century later, except for a few isolated paragraphs and a handful of trade celebrations, the 150th birthday of the domestic oil and gas industry passed virtually unnoticed. Entrepreneurism and its mother—capitalism—now evoke derision, and profit appears to have become profane. And here's the stark contrast: as a nation, we are now importing more than sixty-eight percent of the crude oil we consume,[1] while hundreds of millions of acres of American land, conceivably containing enough petroleum to dramatically reduce our reliance on foreign energy, are blocked from use by drilling bans instituted out of fears based on faulty science. Today, too, the term *oilman* is many flights of stairs down on the respect scale from where it was pre-1970.

At one point in history a citizen's board rejected as too controversial a postage stamp commemorating the 1859 birth of the U.S. oil and gas industry. In 2009, however, not one but a series of four stamps were issued exalting no less an honored symbol of Americanism than the television cartoon series *The Simpsons*.

In this memoir, I hope to capture my adventures through the strange times that fostered this sad reversal of public attitude vis-à-vis petroleum itself—and the people

---

[1] Department of Energy 2009 Statistics

who find it. Beginning in the oilfields of Michigan, my journey has taken me from working as a roughneck in small towns like Ashley, Bloomingdale and Allegan all the way to the legislative halls of Lansing and Washington, D.C., where I served as spokesman for the independent oil and natural gas industry. My odyssey also carried me from living job-to-job to heading up an international oil and gas company. Along the way I sought hard to sharpen my spiritual focus and to maintain dedication to my Christian faith in both my business and personal life. Throughout this book I have included key Biblical verses—passages that have impacted my life and hopefully will be an inspiration to you, as well.

My initial intention of leaving a little story for the grandkids grew substantially when a friend said, "You owe it to everybody who ever started out with nothing but an extraordinary faith in God and in themselves, and refused to compromise their beliefs to tell your full story, John."

By no means is this narrative just about me. It's about us: it's about my wife, Reva, and me, about my brothers, Gene and Jack, and about the extended Miller family, as well—our lives together, our relationship to God, and the good and bad times we have shared.

C. John Miller
Richland, Michigan
Marco Island, Florida

FAMILY FIRST

"Call unto me and I will answer you and show you great and mighty things which you do not know." (Jeremiah 33:3)

  This Biblical verse sums up my seventy-nine years to date. I called to the Lord Jesus Christ very early in life and have sought to conduct myself rightly and fairly. As a result God has blessed me with a lifelong partner and soul mate in my beloved Reva, and has blessed us with our wider family, which has held together in times when many others have fallen apart and dissolved. The oil and natural gas exploration and production business has been good to us Millers, as well, and my professional life has brought recognition, honors and awards beyond my wildest imaginings when we started out "on a rig and a prayer." What successes we have enjoyed are pure testament to our faith in the Lord Jesus Christ.

  I couldn't begin our story without first sharing this secret about "what makes the Millers tick."

THE C. JOHN & REVA MILLER CLAN MEN – 2009. Left to Right, FRONT ROW: Luke Miller, Drew Martin, Nathan Miller, Mike Miller, and Brett Bufton. BACK ROW: Craig Cunningham, Beau Bufton, C. J. Miller, Grant Southwick, Jonathan Southwick, C. John Miller, and Bill Bufton. (Not pictured: Dusty Martin, Jordan Miller, and Peter Loeser.)

THE C. JOHN & REVA MILLER CLAN WOMEN – 2009. Left to Right, FRONT ROW: Whitney Southwick, Ashlyn Bufton, Reva Miller, and Autumn Miller. BACK ROW: Alex Bufton, Sara Miller, Sally Bufton, Pam Miller, Alyson Bufton, Abby Martin, and Cindy Cunningham.(Not pictured: Amanda Miller, Aimee Loeser, A.J. Martin, and Olivia Southwick.)

YES, MICHIGAN IS AN OIL STATE

I have spent all my life around the oil and natural gas exploration and development industry, so it is difficult for me to accept that some folks don't know such an industry exists. Many think of Michigan as just a manufacturing center surrounded by trees and water sitting as an odd-shaped, two-part set of peninsulas encased by four of the five Great Lakes.

Well, it is that. But Michigan is also the fourteenth largest producer of natural gas and the nineteenth largest producer of crude oil of the thirty-four states commercially producing oil and gas. (Sixteen states produce no oil or gas at all.) Michigan is also the sixth greatest petroleum consumer of the fifty states.

The Michigan geological basin was the cradle of the worldwide petroleum industry when in 1858 a hole was hand-dug to thirteen feet in the gum beds of Oil Springs, Ontario, (where Michigan's Dundee Formation reaches closest to the surface) and filled with free-flowing oil. A year later Col. Drake's well at Titusville, Pennsylvania was bored, giving official birth to oil drilling.

Local-use oil and gas wells dotted southeastern Michigan before and after the first-recorded Michigan oilfield was discovered in 1886.[2] The production rates were not spectacular, but it was enough oil to be sold commercially. Michigan had arrived as a real oil and gas producing state.

Over 50,000 holes have been drilled in Michigan to date in the search for oil and gas, resulting in nearly 15,000 oil wells, over 13,000 natural gas wells, more than 3,000 facility wells and over 21,000 dry holes. From less than two percent of Michigan land area, 1.257 billion barrels of crude oil and 6.872 trillion cubic feet of natural gas have been produced from 64 Michigan Lower Peninsula counties.

At this writing, the oil and gas exploration and production industry in Michigan and the United States industry has been paralyzed by indecision, which has brought drilling of new holes to a near standstill. Periods of economic indecision and petroleum exploration slowdown nearly always precede passage of energy legislation. Foremost reason is the knowledge in the industry that legislative energy decisions are made on emotion and political expediency, neither of which bodes well for a capital-intensive speculative industry such as the search for oil and gas.

Public, press and politicos have not learned: the orderly development of oil and natural gas is high tech, low environmentally impactive, and has a safety record of more than ninety-nine percent. A look at drilling and production statistics shows that the more holes you drill, the more oil and natural gas you are likely to find and the production of both begins to climb. Discourage drilling by introducing nebulous and punitive legislation aimed at the people who drill and an energy crisis is bound to follow.

---

[2] Appendix A – Michigan Oil and Gas History

In the United States, scientists tell us that we have only looked in less than two percent of the geographical and geological places that can hold oil and gas. Also, our best recovery methods still only retrieve about thirty percent of the oil and gas in place. Think about that–we've only looked in two percent of the places where oil and natural gas could be, and for every barrel of oil we've pumped, two more are down there.

Following is a good analogy of the petroleum industry at large—according to the Clarke Historical Library's *A History of Michigan Oil and Gas Exploration and Production*:

"Let's say you go to a lake for a day of fishing. While renting a boat you notice that everyone is fishing in one area but another cove is being ignored. 'Why isn't anybody fishing over there?' you inquire, to be told that 'There aren't any fish in that part of the lake. Nobody ever catches anything there.'

"You go over to the ignored part of the lake. The first cast you make into the cove is what in oilfield language would be called an *exploratory* or *wildcat well*. Your first cast catches a fish. That cast is a *discovery well*. You cast again and catch nothing. You've drilled a *dry hole*. You cast again near where you caught the first fish and catch another. The second and third casts are termed *development or field wells* and even though you've had a dry hole, chances are that further casting in the vicinity of the first catch will yield fish, or oil. So you cast again and catch another…and another…and another.

"Soon someone in the group of boats where the 'lake experts' are fishing notices you are catching fish and comes over to fish near you. Since law and courtesy dictate that he not fish in an area within your casting range (or within so many acres of your well), his fishing attempts are offset somewhat from your fishing area and, unless you have fenced off the entire cove for your own use (usually by leasing mineral rights), he starts fishing near you. The newcomer catches fish also. Another fishing boat comes over in your vicinity…then another…and another…with everybody catching fish.

"Eventually a scout for a commercial fishing company happens on this cadre of successful fishers. The firm, **MAJOR**, moves in, gets licenses and fishing rights, launches a fleet of fishing boats and with their vast resources brings state of the art lures and longer fishing poles. It soon dominates the fishing grounds. Some of the folks in the little boats even go to work for **MAJOR**. A cannery is opened at the lakeside and a new and bigger bait shop and boat rental opens, a subsidiary of **MAJOR** called **F**ish **AR**ound **M**y b**O**at **U**nder **T**erms (**FARMOUT**).

"Today for economic, aesthetic and reservoir conservation reasons, wells are 'spaced' by state regulators. This maximizes efficiency and production from a reservoir. Michigan's first well spacing was defined by Public Act 61 of 1939 as a minimum of one well per ten acres. Today in Michigan, well spacing may vary from the minimum 40 acres in shallower fields to 640 acres for the deepest natural gas wells."

MY EARLY YEARS

"Train up a child in the way he should go: and when he is old,
he will not depart from it." (Proverbs 22:6)

My father, Clyde B. (for Beecham) Miller, was born in 1897 in West Virginia. He started in the oilfield when he was twelve, tending boilers that drove the drilling rigs. He grew up in the fields of West Virginia and Kentucky, laboring in those states and later in Michigan.

When Dad began working on the rigs, mechanical equipment was practically non-existent. Horses and mules hauled the heavy equipment; the rest of the work, for the most part, was done by brute force. Also, since there was no transportation (it was impossible to drive back and forth to a drilling job given the state of roads and the lack of vehicles) the men would live in tents out around the well site. They'd wash as water was available, eat as food was available, and work the rest of the time. So it was a tough-tough life. Often Dad worked these fields with his brother George.

My mother was Verna Alexander (Collins) Miller. She was born in 1909. They met when Dad's oilfield life brought him to her hometown of Paintsville, Kentucky. Mom was fifteen when they married in 1924—Dad was twelve years her senior.

Mom and Dad started with an early tragedy: their first child, Carl Ray, died in infancy (February 1927 – April 1927). Their next child was Joan (pronounced Jo-Ann), then Clyde Eugene (after my father), then me, Charles John, (from two cousins in Paintsville, Kentucky—"Charlie" and "John" Brand, who had helped my folks get their business started), then Harry Jack. Last came Janis Belle. Our family of five children and Mom and Dad arrived in Ashley, in central Michigan in 1932. Why there, I'm not positive, but I do know that shortly before they came to Michigan, oil had been discovered on

Verna and Clyde Miller

the eastern side of the state near Saginaw. As that find developed, people began pouring in from states like Kentucky to get involved in Michigan's burgeoning oil and gas business.

I was born September 20, 1931, in Paintsville, Kentucky, dead center in their brood of five. I've never understood what my parents were doing back in my mother's home state of Kentucky when they had moved to Michigan shortly after the Saginaw Oil Field discovery of August 27, 1925. Looking back, I'm convinced a contributing factor behind their return to Kentucky was probably to be close to family during the devastation of the Great Depression. While the vitality of an active oil industry shielded many landowners and communities from the worst of the financial wreckage of the Depression, times were still rough for the independent drilling contractor—the part of the business where Dad and Uncle George worked. Then, as now, drilling contracting was cyclical, and the smaller the contractor, the fewer and farther between were the jobs. And if the contractors had no jobs, neither did Dad, since he worked on the rigs.

Recently I watched the movie *Centennial Man*, set in the 1930s, the decade of my birth. That film, depicting life in those times, hammered home for me the hardship it must have imposed upon my mother and father to have a third child to feed, clothe, and house. No doubt it was difficult for the entire family. The nice part is that I was young and consequently oblivious to the strain of their reality.

A look at the Michigan oil and gas well drilling statistics for that era provides a second clue as to why my family probably headed back to Kentucky for a while. In 1928, there were 283 Michigan permits issued for drilling in search of oil and/or natural gas with 158 holes sunk. In 1929, the year the Great Depression began with the crash of the New York Stock Exchange on October 15th, the state of Michigan issued 576 oil and gas permits, with 483 holes drilled. At that juncture, money for capital investment in the business began to dry up, and in 1930 Michigan permits numbered 257 with 331 holes drilled (many resulting from the high permit number the previous year). In my birth year, 1931, only 111 permits were issued, and only 138 holes drilled. This probably sent Dad and Uncle George scurrying back to the more familiar territory of familial Kentucky…where groceries were more abundant.

ASHLEY

In 1929, Dad and George formed Miller Brothers Drilling Contractors, a company located in Ashley, Michigan—a dot of a city in the center of the Lower Peninsula in Gratiot County, just north of which transpired a lot of drilling in the late 1920s and early 1930s. I suspect the family wanted to locate someplace where they would be close to that high-intensity action, but far enough away from the "boomtown" atmosphere to raise kids in less hectic environs. They could never have suspected that their chosen home county, Gratiot, would become known as a "bone yard," a site of early promise bearing way too little result.

Clyde and George (right) Miller

The Elba Oil Field discovery of 1927—consisting of eight marginal wells— produced a miserly 43,000 barrels of oil its entire lifetime. The Elba Gas Field discovered in 1928— consisting of ten successful completions—produced a paltry 251 million cubic feet of natural gas in its 40-year lifespan. Beyond that, little happened in Gratiot County's production history until mid-1970 when McClure Oil Company drilled Michigan's deepest hole at 17,458 feet.

Fortunately, the Mt. Pleasant Field discovery in 1928 proved that prolific production was indeed possible in central Michigan (562 wells drilled, with 30 million barrels of oil and seven billion cubic feet of natural gas produced). Those discoveries resulted in abundant opportunity for the young Miller family: it meant plenty of work when we returned to Michigan shortly after my birth in 1931.

Huge fields were being uncovered east, west and north of where we were living in Gratiot County. These would be followed in the mid- and latter-'30s by Midland County's *Porter-Jasper Field* in 1933 with 555 wells, 51 million barrels of oil and almost five billion cubic feet of natural gas all time; Isabella County's *Vernon-Rosebush Field* in 1933 with 135 wells drilled, nine million barrels of oil and 440 million cubic feet of natural gas; and Montcalm County's 1935 *Crystal Field*, where 193 holes would produce eight million barrels of oil in its lifetime. More discoveries in the middle of Michigan followed. Dad and Uncle George drilled in a number of those fields.

Looking back, I understand more clearly how the Great Depression had come crashing down on the country, making it sorely difficult for all folks, but especially those with kids. The pleasant—maybe ironic—aspect of this economic pain is the fact that I, as a kid, carried no bad memories of the time, bore no scars. Nor did my four siblings.

We lived in Ashley for a few years. The house was small with no central heating. It had a potbelly, coal-and-wood stove in the front part of the living room. During the cold, winter months, we'd huddle around it to stay warm before heading out to school. There was, predictably, no indoor plumbing either, so we had to trek about twenty yards to a backyard outhouse. When toilet paper wasn't available? A catalog. Pick a section, any section…

At the bottom of the Great Depression, money was scant. If you could live and eat, it was about as good as you could expect. We had a loving and concerned mother and a hard-working father. She was a winsome woman with a keen sense of humor and a heart—a passion—for living out the Gospel. Deep maternal instincts continued to mark her even later in life when she served as exemplary full-time dorm-mother at the Grand Rapids Baptist College (now Cornerstone University) and as premier, part-time matchmaker.

Dad stood about 5'6"—husky and muscular, with one eyebrow light brown, the other pure white. He was quiet, almost reticent by nature, a man whose bearing compelled respect without fear, whose few words were absolute law.

Mother often retold the story about the scar I sport above my left cheek. Our only source of heat was the stove, so all of us kids vied for the space closest to it just to stay warm. One day, she said, I squirmed out of her lap and fell on the open, lower part of the stove, which was hot and also very sharp. It laid open my cheekbone, but my folks figured it wasn't necessary to get stitches, so they pinched the edges together and taped the wound closed. I still carry that mark to this day. I do recall that we would be sitting together on a cold morning, staying awfully close to that stove having hot oatmeal or cream-of-wheat for breakfast as we tried to get warm.

The present economy in the U.S. prompts a comparison of *depression* versus *recession*. By the time I was five years old (1936), the worst of the Depression was over, but times were still hard. It was not unusual to see people going through every drawer of the house or rifling through every pair of trousers, or searching every "whatever" to see if they could find a few extra coins because money was scarce. Extra anything was an oxymoron. Clothes, for instance. You had an outfit—shirt and pants—to wear through the winter; then sometimes you wore them through the hottest part of the summer as well, unless you were lucky enough to have one pair of shorts.

There would be an occasional incident that raised our hackles. Brother Gene—a year my senior—and I once got a little tangled up with our cousin Earl Miller, one of the children born to Aunt Grace and Uncle George. Earl was five years older than us and considerably larger and a whole lot meaner. One taunt inflamed the next and the next as we were outside in the driveway one day and Earl was engaging in his full-blast pestering. Utterly ticked, Gene picked up a small block of wood and hit him cleanly on the back of the head. That whacked a hornet's nest, and an incensed Earl stomped on home.

Ten minutes later Earl bellowed out Gene's name. Gene sneered, "Whaddya want?"

Earl yelled, "My dad wants you and John to come over to the house right now!"

He thought, no doubt, that we were naïve enough to fall for his ruse so he could whip the tar out of us. Instead, we told him to jump in the lake and let it go. It was a typical go-around with bully Earl.

Back Row: Joan and Gene
Front Row: Jack, me, Janis

ASHLEY TO ALLEGAN

When the Bloomingdale Field developed in southwest Michigan, my folks decided to leave the central part of the state and move to Allegan, the headquarters for all southwest Michigan drillers and workers. It was 1937.

Mother's older sister, Bertha, had married Glen Smith, who was also in the oil business, and they moved to Allegan, too. They had one child, Jean, who married Wayne Warren. (Jean still lives in Allegan at this writing.) We got along famously with family on Mom's side.

Uncle Glen worked for Dad for a considerable time and spent virtually all his life in the oil and gas business. I worked with Uncle Glen sometimes—he as a driller, me as a tool dresser. A key, early mentor in my life, he would take me around in the pick-up he drove as superintendent of the drilling crew, and it was he who first taught me how to dress a bit by hitting and pulling it with a sledgehammer in order to reshape it. Uncle Glen was calm and considerate. It was refreshing to have someone of his deportment around, as most of our home was, I confess, loaded up on quick tempers and instant decisions. He imprinted upon me his favorite adage: "The best way to hurry is to take your time."

It was ironic that the Bloomingdale Field would draw me to Allegan, which would become my lifetime hometown. The closeology drilling (wells drilled in tight proximity without legal restriction) in that field led to the enactment of Act 61 of 1939, Michigan's base oil and gas law. How incredible that over the breadth of my professional life—as roughneck, explorer and developer, as a member of the advisory board for the Michigan Oil And Gas Association (MOGA), and as its president—I would deal again and again with the regulations enacted in the Allegan/Bloomingdale boom era and area.

The village of Bloomingdale, in Van Buren County, was established May 23, 1870, along the Kalamazoo and South Haven Railroad. It was originally a lumber center; then after the trees had been harvested, it became an agricultural community. The town's first sixty-eight years were similar to the histories of dozens of small Michigan towns. But all of that changed radically in August of 1938 when a Michigan independent oil and gas exploration and production company, Fisher-McCall, came to town to drill on the Wiggins farm near Bloomingdale.

Allegan County, north of Bloomingdale, began drawing national headlines in 1938 as drilling proliferated with discoveries of oil in southwest Michigan's shallow (1,000 to 1,500 feet) Traverse Formation. In the midst of this widespread publicity, Fisher-McCall received their drilling permit for the Wiggins Estate #1 well with little fanfare. The project, however, soon made banner headlines that dwarfed past newspaper accounts.

In the middle of August, the Michigan Oil & Gas News announced, in double-bold print: "**BARREL A MINUTE WILDCATS OPEN TWO MORE TRAVERSE**

LIME FIELDS," referring to discoveries near Overisel (Allegan County) and Bloomingdale (Van Buren County).

As had transpired in the Crystal Field in Montcalm County a couple of years earlier, the rush erupted, but this time in a small town rather than open land. Leases were signed, permits obtained, and drilling rig crews moved in as life in Bloomingdale shifted into overdrive.

Ultimately the Bloomingdale Field would see 437 wells drilled, 45 of them on 80 acres (less than two acres per well-site) within the village limits,[3] which would produce more than ten million barrels of oil. Practically any space not occupied by people and houses saw a drilling rig sink its roots as people signed leases for mineral rights in their back yard and drillers packed rigs into tightest proximity to each other. More than eleven percent of all wells ever drilled in Michigan—5,400 out of a cumulative total of more than 50,000 statewide—were bored in the neighboring counties of Allegan and Van Buren between 1930 and 1939. Development was so rapid and ruthless in the Bloomingdale Field that oil folks and state regulators jointly agreed on the need for legislation to rationalize and regularize drilling. The result was the fundamental legislation enacted in 1939 (Act 61) that still serves as the basis for the regulation of drilling activity in the state. Even into the late 1940s, there were still about 50 drilling rigs that called Allegan "home," a vestige of the boom that became a whisper.

As with the Crystal Field, so much oil led to refineries. Two built in Bloomingdale—the Erie Refining Company and the Fort-Dalo Oil and Refining Company—reached throughput (refining capacity) levels in the 1,300-1,500 barrels per day range at their peak. These refineries provided hundreds of thousands of gallons of gasoline per month to Kalamazoo district companies and fuel oil to distributors during the rationing period of World War II. Both firms closed their doors in the late 1940s, as oil production dropped, underground water levels rose and economic viability fizzled.

Allegan was a small city on the Kalamazoo River, a town laid out and founded by lumber barons who had made money harvesting stands of the fine timber that existed then in Michigan. They had prospered, and Allegan, as a result, was a thriving community, serving as county seat and offering strong schools. (What a stark contrast to the humble milieu of Ashley.)

My mother faced a monumental problem as we came to Allegan: she had five kids—and a husband in the oil business. Tough combination, enough to sink any ship, and, predictably, she had difficulty finding us a house.

She often told the story of going to many homes seeking a place to rent, only to face the same interrogation: Did she have children? Her response: "Yes…five" became the first black mark.

"And what does your husband do?" was the next—and final—question.

---

[3] This was prior to Act 61 which restricted drilling to no more than one well per ten acres.

When she'd answer that he was in the oil business, the interview came crashing to conclusion, often with the slam of a door.

Then a minor miracle occurred. Mom found a place that just might be available, a large edifice kind of kitty-corner from Dawson Grade School, complete with an enticing playground. A lumber baron had built the home as an engagement gift for his daughter, and it featured lots of imported woods and large rooms.

Mother

As my mother spoke with the lady who owned the house about the possibility of renting, the dark and foreboding question arose: "Any kids?"

"Five," my mother answered.

Here's where grace intruded. "Perfect," the lady said. "Exactly what this enormous place needs—a handful of children."

Mother's follow-up was to ask if she wanted to know how our father made his living, which prompted a second, equally bizarre reply: "If he earns his money honestly, then what he does is none of my business—or interest."

So began the Miller family's extraordinary friendship with Mrs. Sherwood, who lived alone just down the block from us in another large home. We became, I'm convinced, her extended family as we quickly grew to love her. She even seemed to enjoy us kids with all our unbridled energy, but especially little Janis who would head over to her house every Sunday with the newspaper and sit with Mrs. Sherwood while she read.

Six months after we moved in, Mrs. Sherwood approached Mother with what at first blush seemed an outlandish proposal. "Verna," she said, "you can't continue moving these kids around like gypsies. They need to have a solid home, a place to live for an extended period, where they can sink some roots. You, my dear, need to buy this house. You heard me: buy it."

Mother's response was easy logic: "But we can't buy it; we can't afford it."

Mrs. Sherwood said, "Well now, I didn't say how much I wanted, did I? How much could you come up with?"

Mother hesitated, calculating silently. "About $1,900, I think," she finally said, very softly.

"And that," the angelic lady replied, "is exactly what I want for my house."

How wonderful, how incredible for our semi-nomadic family: an immeasurable gift that ensured a degree of stability—a house of our own that allowed us to remain in one place through our school years, a house with a spacious backyard for us would-be athletes where we could shoot baskets and knock around in all our boundless muscle-flexing.

Its interior was constructed of the very best lumber—especially cherry—with a magnificent staircase in the foyer mounting to the second floor, and with sliding doors four inches thick. Residing there anchored our family for the best part of my childhood and decades beyond.

One minor complication was the upstairs layout: five bedrooms and a single bathroom. (Of course it was light years away from that primitive outhouse in Ashley—and its catalogues.) From that upper floor ran a pair of stairways, one descending to the kitchen, the other climbing to the attic, an area with space aplenty for storage, and room left over for our wrestling and boxing matches, all punctuated with early trash-talk.

From the kitchen on the main floor, another stairway dropped to the basement, which housed the furnace and offered additional space for storage. It was there that Mother would stash all sorts of jugs and jars of canned foods for our year-round supply. The garage housed two new cars—a Pontiac coup and a Chevrolet—and had an upper floor for even more storage.

In the backyard towered a number of oak trees with tire swings, a basketball area and a horseshoe pit, and an adjacent driveway with sufficient room for throwing and catching baseballs and footballs as the Miller boys became jocks-for-all-seasons. And if we wanted more exercise, we just hustled across the street to the schoolyard.

We were also only a mile from the Allegan County Fairgrounds, near some of Dad's property that housed his drilling rigs, a few dogs, and even accommodated some riding horses. So, our life changed dramatically for the better in Allegan. In retrospect, I feel profoundly thankful, for at the time I didn't have the brains to understand what kind of upward move my family had just made.

I attended the last half of first grade after we moved into Allegan that spring of 1937. Next fall, I skipped second grade on an asinine technicality: to balance the class counts of second and third, the teachers determined that I should transfer up. I'd already read most of the requisite books for the younger grade, so…in kicked the technicality. Mom consented to the move.

That acceleration, though, left me two years younger than the rest of my class since my birthday fell in September. As a consequence, I eventually ended up beginning high school at twelve and graduating at sixteen. In retrospect, I would have preferred to start my freshman year at fourteen, because that delay would have been a major assist for me athletically. It would have meant extra maturity, extra size.

As I entered the third-grade classroom, the teacher assigned me a seat. I walked down the aisle towards it, and as I passed, one boy snickered, "Think you're smart, don't you?" I didn't have time to respond and just continued to my seat.

At recess, the same boy approached me with another snide remark. From day one the Miller family has carried on our resume that we all possess quick tempers—and mine was set at instant boil. As the kid tried to throw me over, I grabbed his arm, flung him down, and sat on him.

The teacher rushed over and scolded me. "That's not a very good way to start out in a new grade."

Jaw clenched, I responded. "Well, it's either this or letting him sit on me, and I'm not going to do that."

The other boys watched the drama unfold—and all took notes. I had nothing more to prove to any of the third graders, and this one incident quickly came to represent a brand new shot for me—and an instant reputation.

There were three elementary schools in Allegan: the Northward, the Southward, and Dawson, which we attended. The variety made for good competition as each school would play the others in various sports, which were all pick-up games with no adult coaching. We'd just choose teams on our own and play and enforce our own rules. After sixth grade, we moved on to junior high school for seventh and eighth, at which point the guys we'd been competing against became our teammates.

We Miller kids took part in almost every available activity. We didn't have a great deal of money, but many things we loved cost nothing. This was an age before the advent of Little League, Pop Warner, and other adult-structured, adult-dominated, adult-strangled sports. We'd gather as kids at Dawson School for a game of touch football or venture over to the high school where there was grass on which to play tackle. We also had that hoop on the side of the garage in our backyard where we'd play our basketball, perfecting our set-shots. Anybody who wanted to participate showed up, and everybody played. And we ALWAYS kept score! This was way before the popularity of the touchy-feely-Mr.-Rogers mantra that no one should lose. Plus our house was five miles from Little John Lake, which, despite its perpetual chill, was an exhilarating place to swim. To get there, we'd hitch a ride or pedal our bikes.

Dad and Mom ran the house, and everything moved along smoothly, orderly. The essence is that we had a loving family relationship. Like all siblings, there were differences and points of contention from time to time, but be wary if you were an outsider who challenged any one of us Miller kids. Our constitution was simple: if one of us had trouble, the other four would join in, and we needn't sort facts until the outcome was finalized. Our code was in-defense-of-each-other regardless of odds or circumstances. That was particularly true of Gene and me.

After I moved ahead a grade, we had Joan in 5th, Gene in 4th, and me in 3rd. Because we were that close together, we also knew most of each other's friends. Meanwhile, the youngest, Jack and Janis, forged their own set of comrades.

Many times Mom was trying hard to find ways to get us high-octane kids all out of the house. Our home operated on a Spartan-like regimen. Not that we were deprived, we just didn't buy a lot of superfluous things. On the rare occasion Dad would splurge on ice cream, it was the same ritual. He'd buy a gallon and we'd all grab a spoon, sit down and scoop and eat until we hit the bottom of the container. There was, of course, no refrigeration to preserve it anyway.

My maternal grandmother—Granny Collins—would come up periodically from Kentucky by bus, staying anywhere from two to six months with us. By then she was in her 60s, a widow, taller than my mother, slightly rotund, and a marvelous chef who fried everything but the water. She could whip up a meal in short time: chicken, biscuits and gravy, assorted vegetables, salad, and strawberry shortcake for dessert. Hands down, her specialty was chicken—her own Colonel-Collins-Paintsville-Kentucky Fried—with which she even regaled the likes of A.V. and Jon Rex Jones and once dissuaded a police officer from writing a speeding ticket. It was both pleasure and privilege to have her with us, running the kitchen, making the "low-cal" menus.

Every summer, Mother's brothers, Kelly and Bill Collins, would come up from Kentucky. Eventually Bill moved to Michigan. Mother had three sisters, the closest being Bertha.

Dad's sister, my Aunt Hazel, married a guy in the insurance business, Uncle Mack, and they were comfortably set and drove handsome vehicles—Fords and Chevrolets. With no kids of their own, they frequently visited us at Thanksgiving and Christmas and enlivened our holidays with their presence.

When we were young, Gene and I boxed a bit. When Dad was drilling near Bloomingdale, a genuine boomtown back then, he would often take Gene and me there for lunch. Beside the restaurant was a dance-hall/tavern. Dad would bring along the boxing gloves, and after lunch Gene and I would put on an exhibition. Because Gene was the more patient fighter, he beat me up with regularity—something I've never held against my older brother. That was just part of the deal. When Dad passed the hat after our bouts, Gene would receive sixty percent of the take; I would get forty. The typical purse? A couple of bucks.

Eventually I started doing more boxing around Allegan until one day someone proposed I enter the Golden Gloves competition in Kalamazoo. I registered as a light-heavyweight and fared well through a series of matches, whereupon the promoters asked me to move up to the heavyweight division, promising the championship bout would be staged back in Allegan. In my dogged, Milleresque irrationality, I consented only to wind up tangling with a guy who towered 6'5" and weighed 230 pounds—a blue-blood heavyweight. At the end of the fight, the referee called it a draw, which is to say some hometown officiating was alive and flourishing that night six decades ago. Like kissin'-your-cousin maybe—but I celebrated.

From the age of eight, I've always relished the discipline of athletics, and even the rigors and repetition of a systematic exercise program. Back then I'd get up early morning to hit the floor for push-ups and sit-ups. No equipment needed. Just commitment.

I found out later that we were on a tight economic string part of the time. In fact, the guy living across the street, Lem Armintrout, owned the local grocery, and one day I accidentally discovered we were $600 behind on the grocery bill, a problem that deeply concerned my mom. I heard her mention to Mr. Armintrout that we would be taking care of our debt soon.

His response reflected his character. "Hey, I know where you live," he said. "I can see you right across the street; you're not going anyplace; and you need a little assistance. I'm in a position to give that help…forget it." He knew he would get his money eventually, so there was nothing to fret about.

Our situation was common. When the Depression ravaged the country, everyone was wounded financially, and in response, there was a pervasive, helping-hand attitude. Dad aided a number of people when they'd come from the South needing a job by assisting in their hunt. Some of them he'd hire, even creating the work as he could. But it was a very tight line all around.

Still, Mother would somehow scrape up funds if one of us needed clothing for a particular event. Once I thought I needed a suit—which we really couldn't afford—and fortunately she was convinced I needed the suit, too, so she bought one for me, and one for Gene at the same time.

I was the proverbial middle child—locked into the Miller line-up behind Joan and Gene, and ahead of Jack and Janis. In general, the one stuck in the center gets the short end of the stick, and while my case was no exception, I know four siblings who were unalterably convinced I received far better treatment than I deserved.

Mother was the household patrol officer who walked her beat, the basic law-enforcer of Miller Country. If anything arose during the day that needed parental input, she would deal with it. Usually. On rare occasion she'd resort to that cliché about "when your dad gets home." And as kids we weren't eager for the intervention of the Big Billy Goat Gruff. Dad's discipline was all corporal. There was no such nomenclature in our home as a time-out. Instead, there were switches we'd cut ourselves that he would then apply with heavy strokes to our backsides. Of course, Gene was cunning enough to select a slightly cracked branch so when Dad lashed him with it, it'd break. Gene was always quickest at finding his way out of desperate straits.

Dad's manual remedy to problems didn't end with the switch. He took a similar, heavy-handed approach to a sports injury I once sustained. I was behind the plate catching a baseball game in Kalamazoo when the batter tipped a pitch into my right (throwing) hand, fracturing my middle finger and splitting off most of its nail. We had no subs, so I—hardcore commando to the last inning—stayed in despite the pain and despite the blood that leaked onto the balls, which required periodic replacement.

Afterwards, I drove back to Allegan, grimacing all the way, my hand throbbing. Once home, I showed the injury to Dad. "John, I know exactly how to treat that," promised Dr. Clyde, who proceeded to pour scalding water into a bowl, stir in Epsom Salt, place his hand on top of mine, and submerse them both as he pressed down tight. I fought back twin impulses to scream and run. I never did have that finger reset—just left it to heal on its own. And today? Still crooked. Still a reminder…

MY CHRISTIAN FAITH

In Ashley, we did attend a church, but I was too young to remember much. When we moved to Allegan, we lived a short distance from Allegan First Baptist. Of course, we were also just a hop away from the Presbyterian, the Methodist, the Catholic and the Bible churches, too, as all lay within a space of three blocks.

Immediately we began attending First Baptist. Reverend Ezra R. Hill was a strong Bible-based pastor. There were vigorous youth programs, dedicated Sunday school teachers, and excellent preaching. Basically, if the church doors opened, we Miller kids were there, including Sunday school, and Baptist Young People's Union (BYPU). (Of course if we really didn't want to go, we accentuated the "PU" part of it.) In any event, the church became an integral part of our lives, our home-away-from-home.

My mother came to know the Lord during our early years there, which made a telling difference in her life. She soon became an intense student of Scripture and took Moody Bible Institute correspondence courses to enhance her theoretical understanding of the Word of God and to make practical its application. She blossomed spiritually and started using our home as a place to bring in oil industry people for dinner; afterwards she'd take them to services. Dad remained disinclined to participate in anything pertaining to church. On rare occasion—and as a concession to Mom—he would attend special meetings with our guests, but this happened sporadically and never reflected a sincere desire on his part to be there.

There was always a decided difference between Mom and Dad's views of Christianity. Dad was uninterested in church, utterly obstinate about attending. Looking back—and I'm not being critical—I'm convinced Mom so desperately wanted him to become a believer that she probably badgered him into occasionally losing patience. I just think such spiritual pressure may have worked against her desire.

As children, we all came to know the Lord Jesus in church. In my case, summer Bible school provided the turning point. I remember where I, at seven, sat as my teacher, Thelma McGrew, led us in the study of various passages, including: *"For God so loved the world, that he gave his only begotten Son, that whosoever believeth in him should not perish, but have everlasting life." (John 3:16)*

Mrs. McGrew challenged each of us to get to know Jesus as Lord and said, "It isn't something that you all of a sudden put on and wear. It is a decision you make, a decision you acknowledge, if in no other way than at least in prayer, by asking God to allow you to become a part of His family by accepting Jesus Christ as your personal Savior."

So she led me in that prayer, and shortly afterwards Gene and I were baptized together at First Baptist there in Allegan. That decision, that prayer, jump-started me on the journey I'm still on today seven decades later.

Overall, our church life created an affirming atmosphere and reinforced a value system as I grew up, and when I got older, I became involved in the young people's group not because Mom wanted me to be active, but because I desired to be there and because I wanted to share the gospel with others. Every Sunday morning we'd even drive our car like a taxi around the community of Allegan and bring six to ten friends to services with us.

With five kids swarming around her, and with Dad working away much of the time, Mom found Sundays the perfect time to seek a little respite. It was then that she'd occasionally hand us some change so we could walk to the movie theater for a matinee. One Sunday as we passed the church, the pastor and his wife were changing the letters on the sign out front. They questioned us.

"Where are you kids headed?"

We explained we were going to the show. They proceeded to tell us how, in our faith, movies were not acceptable and that the theater was an improper place for us. One of us (I swear it wasn't me) naively repeated this conversation to Mom. End of our shows.

At fourteen I made a commitment to read the Bible all the way through in one year, a venture that stretched and grew me spiritually, and also prompted me to pose many questions of Mom, our pastor, and even an occasional guest speaker. I still strive to read a portion of scripture daily as I seek to deepen my understanding of God's vision for the world and to grasp the responsibility I have as His ambassador.

I can't over-emphasize how critical our family and church experiences were. We kids learned to do right; we learned there were penalties and consequences for messing up; and we learned we needed to grow in the things of God in those spiritual precepts foundational to a life of faith.

"Children, obey your parents in the Lord, for this is right. 'Honor your father and mother' — which is the first commandment with a promise— 'that it may go well with you and that you may enjoy long life on earth.'" (Ephesians 6:1)

RAISED IN THE MICHIGAN OIL PATCH

People are always surprised to find out just how complex the oil and gas exploration and production business is and are invariably shocked to discover how little the guy whose name is on the well really owns. Independent oil and gas explorers round up investors with the hopes of drilling a successful oil and/or natural gas well, knowing chances are about one-in-ten of hitting commercial quantities of oil or gas, and just one-in-fifty of discovering a new field.

Drilling contractors, like Dad and Uncle George, were among the dozens of outside support-services and supply-outfits that explorers and producers hire to perform specialized operations involved in drilling the hole and—if they are lucky—producing the resultant well. Such contractors are the entrepreneurs who own the rigs and hire them out to drill holes for the producers and explorers. Sometimes these contractors will accept a portion of the proceeds from the well—if successful—in lieu of, or as a portion of, their drilling fee, a risky, but sometimes rewarding, practice. In the end we ran the soup-to-nuts: from geology to syndication to drilling to production.

In addition to gathering syndicates of investors, producers/operators manage the wells—whether they've drilled them, or bought them as producing properties. In the mid-1940s, Uncle George purchased some producing wells near Bloomingdale and opted to supervise their production. His decision to leave the roving life of the drilling business meant he and Dad would go separate—albeit amicable—ways. Dad continued in the drilling business under his own name: "Clyde Miller, Contractor."

All of his life Dad labored in the oilfields, doing tough work often in remote, inhospitable and lonely places under torturous conditions, in an environment where ambition, integrity and self-reliance are the most indispensable utilities in life's toolbox, an environment hard and unforgiving that challenges the talents and integrity of a person, leaving no room for excuses, extending no patience to those who fail to get the job done right. Those elements shaped and imprinted my father.

Dad was stern, and you had to earn his respect, regardless of biology or proximity. When he decided you had what it took, he was behind you all the way and showed you grace. Conversely, when you goofed up, his response was just as ferocious in the opposite direction. Dad's hard-line, uncompromising curriculum to teach us kids how to survive in life and in the workplace was simple: "Kick 'em off the end of the dock." He was a tough-tough taskmaster, short-of-temper, but fair in judgment. And I owe him this: he kicked me repeatedly off that dock until I learned how to swim.

Once, when I was twelve, Dad needed some drill-pipe work done at Spang & Company in Mt. Pleasant (about 140 miles north of Allegan). He decided I was going to drive that pipe up to Mt. Pleasant, so I took my friend Richard Smith along to ride shotgun. By then I had been driving for quite awhile, but just at drill sites and on short runs around Allegan. I was scared to death at the prospect of such a long trip behind the steering wheel.

Still I knew "I don't think I can do it" never floated a boat in Dad's marina.

He worked on the unswerving principle that he wouldn't ask you to do a job if he thought you couldn't handle it, and your own doubts about your capabilities were your problem, not his. Maybe that sounds harsh, but it occurs to me that it really tied in, on a different plane, with my accepting Jesus Christ as personal savior and finding out that God Himself promises not to give you anything that He doesn't provide you a way to succeed. Dad's wasn't a religious perspective, so I'm not sure how he'd cotton to my comparing life lessons he taught me with precepts I learned in church. Hopefully, it would make him smile…

Anyway, Rich and I set out for Mt. Pleasant.

There were no turn signals on the truck, so when you drove, you would open the window, thrust out your left arm and point in the direction you were planning to turn. We reached Mt. Pleasant after six hours of white-knuckled driving on two-lane roads, then had to wait while Spang did its work. Richard and I were so exhausted, our energy so utterly spent, that we headed to Mt. Pleasant's Island Park and slept for a few hours. Later that same night the Spang folks helped us load and secure the materials, which we drove back to the drilling location—safely.

My first long-haul trip was behind me, and I was flying high on the hubris of getting the job done right and on the joy of having earned Dad's respect.

REVA JEAN

"Whosoever findeth a wife findeth a good thing,
and obtaineth favour of the Lord." (Proverbs 18:22)

The most significant—serendipitous—part of my early school experience was meeting a young lady in the first grade by the name of Reva Pickitt. We also knew each other because the Pickitt family attended First Baptist and we were in all of the same groups together. And so commenced an incredible relationship that has continued to grow stronger and deeper to this day.

I know what it was that first drew me to her back then, some seven decades ago, and has held me ever since. It was her full-of-fun nature, her independence and athleticism (she was her father's *"son"*), and the interests and inclinations we've always shared. Over the next decade, our friendship tightened, eventually morphing into a love far beyond friendship. She became, of all things bound on earth, my richest blessing.

As we moved into high school, Reva knew a lot of Gene's friends, and later she would tell me that several of the girls would approach her asking, "What are the Miller boys doing?" "Who do Gene and John like?" and "Who don't they like?" Typical, sophomoric stuff. Then she would come to us and say how *so-and-so* was interested. This continued until finally she was talking to me about some matter, and I remember thinking that rather than her coming to me with names of girls who might be interested in me, that I was really most interested in knowing more about her. No more the intermediary.

In truth, from first grade on, Reva was always in my life, with much of our earliest time together marked by teasing and humor. She and her girlfriends (especially Kay Meyers) would have slumber parties at her house only to sneak out around 4 a.m. to make a run first on the bakery, then to hustle over to our place to awaken Gene and me, fast asleep on the back screened-in porch, and not with gentle nudges, mind you, but with raucous hollering. I know in time that Reva's mother discovered—to her full-blown chagrin—her daughter's dawn-breaking antics.

One night Reva also helped orchestrate another prank, this one resulting in my introduction to lawyers. She and her buddy Kay, along with George Whitney, knew I was out on a date with another Reva (Reva Morris), spotted my car and started chasing after us. Suddenly a horse materialized in the middle of the road, and though I tried to swerve, I couldn't avoid the impact, plowing into the animal, crippling it, and doing major damage to the front of Dad's car, as well. Within minutes the owner of the horse was in my face, full of fury, threatening to sue.

That's when Dad interceded, but with advice only: to confer with an attorney whose name he suggested. That was my father's wisdom: to have me, not him, talk to the lawyer—which I did. My first legal counsel was to explain to the farmer how the accident was not my fault at all, but his, for failing to keep his horse fenced in. That tack defused the situation; in the end, we settled amicably with zero damages on either side. Even back then, Reva thought it was funny.

We started dating at a young age: I was a sophomore; she was a freshman. I even gave her some Evening in Paris perfume for Christmas. So we would date some; then she would date others; then I would date others; then we would date each other again… It cycled back and forth like this, although we mutually considered each other #1 even in the course of our dating others.

Reva's parents, Harry and Wilma (called Ann) Pickitt, were raised in the general area of Pullman, a tiny town towards the Lake Michigan shore and about ten miles west of Allegan. When Harry dated Wilma the first time, they went out in a horse and buggy. Harry was an industrious guy who started out by working on roads. His company used hand tools and what was called a horse-drawn scraper pan, which was tied to the horse by a harness that allowed you to drop the blade of the scraper and take a little cut—but not very deep lest the horse not be able to pull it. You'd put that scraping on the pan, have the horse walk to where you would dump it, then come back and do it again and again and again. That and a hand shovel was the way they started building roads back then. By the time we moved to Allegan in 1938, Harry's business was accelerating, as he would acquire plots of land with his keen eye for developing their sand and gravel content which he then sold for the building of roads, airports, etc.

Wilma and Harry Pickitt – Ft. Lauderdale, Florida

Harry taught Sunday school, was on the board of First Baptist, and was recognized as a leader in both industry and community. Wilma was an easy person to love—an encouraging, compassionate, and modest woman. She was just awfully good to me. What I admired most about her and Harry was their open-handed generosity.

In addition to owning a stately home in Allegan, they also bought a beautiful cottage on Gull Lake when Reva was nine, and from then on, it was there the Pickitts would spend every summer, from school's end to Labor Day. The structure featured five bedrooms, a pair of baths, a medium-sized kitchen and a spacious living room highlighted by a stone fireplace. But there was no furnace, so when a cold snap hit, they sometimes scrambled for coal to fend it off.

It was on the lake that Reva best demonstrated her competitive and athletic spirit, which sometimes bordered on recklessness. More than once she and I would venture out in her row boat with its small motor to meet up with Kay Meyers and Ralph Boe in the bay, where we'd square off, power up, then charge at each other, like jousters, only to veer aside at the last moment to avert a collision. We would laugh and laugh, daredevils on the high seas of Gull Lake. Out there, we avoided calamity, but Reva did succeed in sinking that little rowboat of hers—when she pretended its seating capacity was eight highly animated, giggling girlfriends. Harry was less than jovial.

Reva's mom never really liked the lake—had, in fact, a fear of the water, which she sought to camouflage from her children. And Reva's sisters didn't share her passion and exuberance for Gull Lake. Shortly after Wilma passed away Harry gave the cottage to Reva (the other sisters—Wid, Miriam and Lois—received commensurate shares in cash), and the beat went on, the Pickitts' tradition continuing with the next generation of Millers as we raised our four kids with the identical summers-at-the-lake calendar.

In 1980, after Harry and Wilma had both died, Reva and I decided to raze the cottage and build our year-round home on the site. Reva's approach to the demolition was no-nonsense, no-sentiment: "It didn't bother me at all—the tearing down. So what, right?" But her sisters were another matter. All three drove out from Allegan and sadly watched the dismantling.

I have strong, grateful memories of Reva's mother. A gracious, gentle lady, Wilma frequently drove her Cadillac out to the homes of folks living on the margin to deliver food and clothing to get them over some economic hump. And she never performed her acts of charity in a way that was either noisy or condescending, never viewed herself as big shot coming to see a poor person. She was just a loving Christian sharing her blessings from God with others less fortunate. It was spiritual magic watching her heart at work.

She had a tradition too that when someone joined First Baptist, she would arrange a dinner in her home after a Sunday night service and invite three or four couples to welcome these new folks as church members. Harry and Wilma were exceptionally good leaders, unswervingly consistent in their Christian walk, genuine role models worthy of emulation.

I got to know the character of Wilma one day when I was just a sophomore. I'd ridden out to Gull Lake with my sister Joan and gone out into the water to swim with Reva and some other kids and to try our hand at water skiing. All at once I became profusely sick, fighting dizziness and an urge to vomit as I headed into the cottage. Wilma (Mrs. Pickitt to me then) said, "John, why don't you lie down in the guest room here and rest. You'll feel better soon."

So I lay down and immediately fell into a deep sleep. Next thing I knew I was awakening to find Mrs. Pickitt sitting on the side of the bed feeling my forehead. I was lying there in my undershorts—which to modest, teenaged me was virtually naked. I grabbed a blanket, trying to cover myself, utterly embarrassed.

Mrs. Pickitt said, "John, relax. I have seen a lot of young boys in their underclothes; don't make some big deal out of this."

I have never forgotten her poise and benevolence. Here I was, making a terrible impression, certainly not at my best, but her instinctive kindness exceeded all my humiliation. She and I got along swimmingly. In fact, she spoiled me.

Reva was one of four in the Pickitt sorority. Her oldest sister is called "Wid," for "Wilderene." She married Chuck Sheffer who had followed his father into the grocery business after coming home from World War II. Then he started a cheese business on the side and, in the end, cheese turned out to be his primary enterprise, which flourished there in Allegan. Wid and Chuck's kids are Roxie, Ron, Mark and Debbie. When Chuck died, Wid moved to Richland, where she still resides at the age of 86.

Reva's next sister, Miriam, married Boone Cook, who followed his relatives into the oil and gas drilling, contracting and development business, just like my dad then, and like me in time. They had a trio of kids: Brent, Ann and Jeff. Tragically, Boone died in his early forties, leaving Miriam to raise the family as a single parent, which she did with admirable dexterity. Miriam passed away in January 2005.

Reva's younger sister, Lois, married a Naval person named Bill Smith (my mother was the matchmaker), and together they raised a pair of kids: Cassie and Wes. We remain close to all on the Pickitt branch.

The Miller side proved equally prolific. Joan and her husband, Emery Johnson, had three children: Linda, Julie and Rick. Gene and Betty raised four kids: Kelly, David, Danny and Sue. Jack and Phyllis produced a full hand: Jack Jr., Pam, Larry, Sharon and Ron. And Janis and her husband, Dale Orr, nurtured another quintet: Kathy and Brenda, twins Trevor and Travis, and Abby.

Formidable numbers, generation upon generation, as the Pickitts and Millers, in combination, became an army of students marching through the Allegan School system. Nor was it any different at First Baptist, where a parishioner once noted, "We have learned one thing here: never make a derogatory comment about anyone in this church because they are all related in some fashion or another."

That wasn't far from the truth because as the network expanded, the Goodwin clan got grafted in as well. Harry's sister Dessie married into the Goodwin family—they were in the road and bridge building business. They purchased their sand and gravel inventory from Harry's company.

Reva was raised in a genteel manner. Even during these tight financial times she was able to have things she desired such as new clothes, records, etc. After graduating from high school, Reva started college at Taylor University, but didn't care for that school and transferred to Hope College while still a freshman. At the end of her sophomore year, we had a series of discussions about maybe getting engaged, then getting married.

I don't know how keen she really was about the notion. I joke that she sort of took me on as a mission project. We became engaged in June and got married three months later. There was a reason for our wedding date of September 22, 1951: Reva became twenty on June 1st; I became twenty on September 20th. And she insisted that our wedding announcement reflect we were both twenty, not that she was twenty and I a younger nineteen. So we exchanged our vows two days after my twentieth birthday.

We have been married now nearly six decades, and I must say it is wonderful just to be here and be able to tell this story. On January 22, 1982, when I was fifty, I had a coronary blockage that cost me about 40% of my heart. At that point, I figured God was trying to tell me something about the weight and stress of my work schedule by shooting a warning shot across my bow. I knew I would rather be alive with my family than traveling the world and hastening my demise, so I slowed down. Following a second heart attack in 1994, I had quadruple by-pass surgery. Now, here we are in 2010, and I am still above ground, loving and being loved by God and by my family. For me, that's as good as it gets!

God has lavished immeasurable grace upon us, and Reva and I have had the pleasure of seeing our children born: Mike (1954), Cindy (1956), Sara (1958), Sally (1960), and watching them grow up to become spouses, parents, and grandparents. Our little family of six now numbers thirty-three [4] with more additions pleasantly anticipated. We thank God past all measure and beyond all words for the life He has allowed us to lead.

---

[4] Appendix B – John and Reva Miller Family

MY HIGH SCHOOL SENIOR YEAR

I had a generally enjoyable experience in the Allegan school system with good teachers and fast friends. I played football, basketball and baseball in high school, winning my earliest varsity letter in baseball at thirteen. At fourteen, I played varsity football as a linebacker and center, and the next year I was elected captain of the Allegan team and was named an All-Conference selection at season's end.

Gene and me - Allegan High Football

Unfortunately, my senior year in high school turned out to be a debacle. I had tons of extra-curricular stuff going on as captain of the football team and president of the student council—and I got a little full of myself, rather arrogant in fact. I even figured, in my temporary insanity, that I didn't really have to go to school since I needed just a credit and a half to graduate. So I attended only two classes.

I absolutely squandered the academic year, never studying, just letting my grades (the few I got) slide. Afternoons I had a single class, then frittered time in the garage banging away on the punching bag before heading back to school for whatever sport was in season. I believe now I was uncertain about my future and just didn't know what I wanted to do. So I acted out my frustration in unhealthy ways.

One situation in baseball best exemplified my overbearing, hair-trigger temperament at that time—and featured the collision of an immature, fourth-year athlete with a strong-armed, uncompromising coach. I knew Coach Bob Peckham well, knew that he was a World War II veteran with an explosive temper. He stood 6'5" and was heavily muscled, extremely athletic. In college he'd had a glittering career as a gritty, in-your-face basketball player.

Come spring, he coached baseball at Allegan. In one particular game, Coach Peckham didn't start senior me. Instead he had the audacity to insert into the lineup a player with a lower batting average. I figured he'd play me after a couple of innings, but he didn't. Finally enough was enough, so I left the dugout, walked to the locker room, showered, changed clothes and scooted home.

That evening I got a call from a good friend who said, "Boy, Coach is really mad at you."

"What about?" I asked.

He said Peckham had called for me to go into the game. Then he yelled again for me, and my friend told him I wasn't there.

"Well, where is he?" Peckham screamed.

My friend said he'd seen me walking toward the locker room.

Next morning Coach Peckham pounded into study hall and told me in unequivocal terms that he wanted me in his classroom—right now. We marched there together, and he locked the door behind us—actually locked it. I knew ex-marine Peckham had a history of fighting with students, so I was wary and on-guard as I sat down in a chair and he wedged his goliath frame behind his desk.

"I am disappointed in you," he began. "Very disappointed."

He looked hard at me.

"And I am very disappointed in you," I said, trying to hold his stare.

All at once he jumped up and slammed his fist on the desk, scattering a dozen books. I thought he was coming over the top right after me, and I didn't know whether to block him with the chair or run.

Finally, he gathered some restraint, sat back down and said, "I am not going any further with this; I am just going to stop it right now. You, sir, are off the team."

"I figured that out last night," I told him. "Besides, I'm taking a job and will be working from four in the afternoon to midnight."

He said, "You're going to do WHAT?"

"I'm going to work—in the oil field—so this is going to be perfect for me," I said as I scrambled to my feet and fled the room.

My Allegan High School
senior picture

My dad had been drilling a well by Burnips—which was about a twenty-mile ride from home. He needed somebody on the evening shift, so I did indeed have a job and proceeded to work those hours until my graduation.

At first, I wasn't even going to attend the graduation ceremonies, angry as I was with how my senior year had wound to its egregious close. But after encouragement from Reva, I relented and was there to pick up my diploma.

So ended my high school days.

Let me tack on a footnote to the Bob Peckham saga. Over a decade later, I served on the Allegan Board of Education when he applied to become superintendent of schools. Of course, everyone on the board knew Bob's lengthy history of being confrontational, even draconian, with students and athletes. (As I could attest.) But I'd watched him change dramatically over the years, noticed how self-control had replaced volatility. Long gone were the days he'd lay those huge hands on students in anger. So I lobbied hard for his candidacy for superintendent—a job he won, and discharged admirably up to his retirement many years later.

In 2009 when Reva and I came back to Michigan for the summer, I sat down for lunch with Bob and spent the most pleasant afternoon with him, replaying the dusty reels from our past, recalling the rocky start from which our friendship grew. His was almost a redemption story, I thought. And there we were, well over half a century later, laughing, relishing each other's company. I was 77. Bob was 93.

OUT OF HIGH SCHOOL …
INTO THE WORKING OIL FIELDS

At the time of my ignominious departure from the halls of Allegan High School at the age of sixteen in June of 1948, Dad had a rig running up north of Muskegon, so he sent me up there to work with an old, leathery fellow named Frank Seifert, a driller, with me alongside as an exceedingly green tool-dresser. A key reason Dad sent me was that Frank had a drinking problem, a suspended driver's license—and zero transportation. My father set me up with his old Pontiac and assigned me the job of picking Frank up, leaving early enough on Monday morning to arrive at the rig by 7:30 a.m. I'd stay in Muskegon through the week to get home late Saturday evening for a truncated weekend.

We ended up in a flea-bag of a motel and Dad in his frugality insisted we rent only one room between us. With Frank in tow, I drove back and forth to the rig from that motel, which also meant when we finished up in the evening, he would want to go wherever I was headed for dinner. Consequently, I couldn't meet anybody during my off-hours. Once I did decide to go to the roller rink, and Frank insisted upon tagging along. I might as well have just read a book, I figured. Overall, though, Frank was an interesting character, just not a guy I wanted to spend wads of time with!

Other frustrations abounded. A key one was the nasty location of our job site—about half a mile over a steep hill, then back along the riverside. To get down that hill was a serious task because when it started snowing, we couldn't drive closer than three-quarters of a mile to the rig—so we had to walk in and then walk back out.

In truth, I learned a lot from Frank Seifert despite the tension that occasionally revved our competitive juices. I knew I was in exceptional physical condition at this time. Frank and I would take the drilling bit (heavy piece of steel) off the end of the tool that was at the bottom drilling the hole (the bit would wear down from the extreme friction). We would have to unscrew the drill bit and use a chain hoist to put it into the fire. We'd then replace the bit and continue with the drilling. Frank's principal responsibility was to pay attention; mine was to get that bit into the forge and stoke that fire until you had red-to-white-hot steel. Then I had to bring the bit up out of the forge, swing it around and position it on the anvil. Frank would take a sledgehammer on one side, and I'd take a sledge on the other. We then had to dress the bit, meaning we had to pull steel from its center out to the edges by virtue of hitting that bit just right with those hammers … thus shaping it.

Frank was big and strong with muscles like rope and vice-like hands, and he wanted to make sure I understood that he was inarguably tougher than I was, and I—Miller through and through—wasn't eager to accept that assumption. We would go after that bit as hard as we could, hoping the other one would set down his sledgehammer first to take a breath—a kind of flag of surrender. It got to be an Olympic duel!

One time as we were heavily engaged in combat, Dad and Gene drove up, and watched us slam away at that bit and at each other's ego. Short-fused Dad got madder and madder, then yelled at us, "Idiots! You guys are hammering on cold steel…you can't get anything done that way, and you both know it. Now stick that bit in the forge, heat it up, and get back to work."

Still, those contests would arise from time to time, all comprising an invaluable experience for me, my hands-on practicum as I began to learn the basics of the oil business up close and personal.

COLLEGE ... SORT OF ...

But Mom had other ideas for Gene and me that did not involve the oil fields of Michigan: she wanted both of us to go to college. The summer of 1948 Gene and his buddy Jim Andress hitchhiked to Texas and secured jobs out there working on oilfield equipment. He returned to Allegan that September, and Mother again broached the idea of college. Actually, it was far more than a suggestion as she had already enrolled us at Bob Jones University. Neither of us knew much about the school, but Mother could be exceedingly persuasive, and she worked overtime drawing up this set of blueprints. In the end, she and Aunt Bertha escorted Gene and me down to Greenville, South Carolina, for our matriculation.

Naturally, we were not keen on going, but Mother was full of maternal insistence. Once there, we received room assignments, I in one, Gene in another.

We said, "No way...we're rooming together."

They said, "No, we don't put brothers together."

We informed them that we were leaving if we couldn't be roommates, until finally they conceded, which meant five students in one room—with a single sink. Thus began our year at Bob Jones, an ultra-conservative school with a tight, constricting, suffocating structure.

For example, there was in attendance at Bob Jones a young lady named Mary Robbins from Bangor (near Allegan) whom I knew vaguely. After dinner one night I spotted her outside and reintroduced myself. We chatted. She was pleasant and attractive, and I offered to walk her back to her dormitory. She agreed. Later, when I returned to my room, our trio of upper-class roommates confronted me, asking where I'd been. I thought, what's it to you? but said, "I walked a young lady to her residence hall."

One responded, "YOU DID WHAT?" I calmly repeated my explanation.

"Well, you can't do that here," he said, his voice rising. "After the dinner hour, there is NO way a guy and gal can be together except at the furniture parlor where they have a number of faculty people seated as chaperones. You can sit there to visit with one another; but then she goes back to her dormitory alone, and you come back to your dormitory alone."

I thought, Whoa, we've landed in a penitentiary here. It's Alcatraz.

That was the beginning of the Miller brothers' fast slide away from Bob Jones, but to keep ourselves from going wacko, we assembled a basketball team. The rule there was that you could play until you got beat, so we tried to be on the floor first after the evening meal, then kept track of how many times we could make it all the way through the night without losing. Even though Gene and I weren't the best basketball players, we had played enough to know talent and strategy, so we selected three other exceptional athletes and one solid substitute and assembled an extremely strong team there at Bob Jones Alcatraz U.

Come Christmas break, Gene and I headed home with one resolution: that our first semester would also be our last. So, after the holidays we drove Dad's car back to South Carolina, parking it in an obscure corner just off school grounds. Need I mention: having a car on campus violated another rule...

But leaving that car idle while we checked off the calendar was just too tempting, and on occasion we'd sneak off and tool around Greenville, soaking up its secular, southern culture, then pull back into our inconspicuous spot, just biding our time, counting down the exam days, waiting impatiently for the hour we could pack it all up and trek north.

Unfortunately, one day Gene was pushing too hard on the pedal, which inspired a local policeman to pull us over to the curb—aggressively, I should add. Wagging his ticket book, he began to berate us for "speeding in the city limits...you northerners with that Michigan plate..." Then he asked the question that would free us. "Just what are ya'll doin', anyway?" he drawled.

We explained we were brothers, both freshmen at Bob Jones, waiting to take our finals, that we would then be heading back to Michigan—for good. Suddenly his deportment did a reverse pivot, and he started chuckling as he shook his head from side to side. "Boys," he said, "I'm not going to write you up because you're both in enough trouble already. Now git on back to that campus." We thanked the cop and headed off, full of caution. It was obvious: the community of Greenville knew fully well the rigidity of its local college.

In truth, all our extra-curricular zeal—especially the athletics—never carried over to the classroom. Reva insists Gene and I were kicked out at semester's end, but we truly weren't. We left of our own volition, and the dean of men even told us if we ever wanted to come back, Bob Jones University would be glad to have us. No way do I pretend he was being honest, but he did make that comment nonetheless.

That was the first time I had ever begun to think about people being tied up with way too many Rules–Rules–Rules imposed on students just to exercise Control–Control–Control. Anyway, the Miller brothers' inability to comply with punitive regulations, plus our propensity toward the physical rather than the cerebral, led to our abrupt departure from the school.

Later, as natural gas explorers/developers, Gene and I continued to resist what were flagrantly ridiculous rules and oppressive regulations. The big difference was that by then we had matured and learned to work within the system, to the point that we could even introduce some logic into regulation. Behind the diplomacy, however, our intolerance for injustice remained. And apparently that constitutes a family trait, because younger brother, H. Jack, showed the same inclination and determination, which became most evident later on in our battle over the Nordhouse Dunes.

Bottom-line: at the end of the first semester, Gene and I headed back up north to Michigan, leaving Bob Jones University in the rearview mirror, and started into the oil business full-time. It was February, 1949.

41

BACK TO THE OILPATCH

In the spring of that year, Dad had an opportunity to procure some better equipment. The rigs he had then were wooden and awfully bulky, so we had to pay an outside company to come in and move the large structures. Each had a fifty-foot wooden mast that lay out in one piece, so we had to tie a trailer clear to the back of it and rest the front section on our truck, all of which meant that we'd have to navigate the roads dragging behind us something over sixty feet long. Think about corners.

Back then we never even considered load weight. Dad's theory was that you stacked the trucks until nothing was left on the ground, that when you left a site, you were taking everything. So we would often inch down the road grossly overloaded.

After I'd started working for my father again, we were drilling up around Sparta one time and while I was home for an abbreviated weekend, he asked me what I thought about how something should be done on the rig. "What are you asking me for?" I said sarcastically. I was dead tired and fully disgusted being the kid on the crew, low man on the proverbial totem pole, all the while absorbing constant ribbing for being the boss's son, though by then I knew more than most of the drilling crew and had decidedly more experience understanding exactly how he wanted the work done. "I'm the least paid person you have on that rig."

Gutty statement to my dad—and probably naïve. I was convinced I'd played one too many cards. But Dad never said a word. He just rose and left the room, and I thought, well there goes my job. Five minutes later he returned and handed me $200—which was like $2,000 today.

"Now, when you get back up there," he said, "you tell them you are in charge." Great, I thought. Those guys are really going to pay attention to a kid.

"Oh," he added "and take your brother Jack up there with you and start teaching him how to dress a bit."

It is a tribute to Dad's native management instincts that he had Jack go with me back to where I was to take command. He knew I needed someone greener than myself on the job, and Jack would be willing to follow my lead rather than question orders and put me down.

With that, I became a tool pusher[5] and Dad had equipped me with at least one person I could boss with implicit authority. He knew, too, that the rest of the men would fall in line. And he was right: they all did.

---

[5] A term used to designate authority on drilling equipment and among drilling personnel.

INTO THE NAVY AND BACK HOME

In 1950, the Korean War put oilfield manpower and equipment into short supply, creating a decline which adversely impacted everyone involved in U.S. domestic oil and gas drilling. The whole situation looked ominous to me—laboring in the oilfield as I was at the time—and I was beginning to feel the economic pain. Older brother Gene joined the Navy, but a childhood bout with rheumatic fever had so weakened his system that he received an early discharge.

I joined the U.S. Navy Reserves in the early 1950s and was called up to full-time service in March of 1952. By then I had formulated a new plan for when I re-entered civilian life, and it would not be back into the economic quicksand of a fickle oil and gas business. No way. I intended to do something far more stable: I would work for my father-in-law in the sand and gravel business. (Though time and circumstance would soon enough scuttle that game plan.)

U.S. Navy - 1952

I went to Navy boot camp at Great Lakes Naval Station in Illinois and became a Chief Recruit Petty Officer, which meant I had Saturdays and Sundays off—very rare for a recruit—so Reva was able to drive from Michigan for the weekends.

In short time I was assigned to the Seabees, the Construction Battalions (CB's) of the U.S. Navy, whose job description was simple: build bases, bulldoze roadways, erect bridges, and create airstrips … anything and everything construction-related in military theaters of operation.

Then I headed off to Port Heuneme, California, for training while Reva remained in Michigan. When I arrived on base, a message was waiting, informing me Dad had suffered a heart attack. I received immediate leave to fly back to Allegan. There I found my father looking okay, but wearing a concern I'd never seen before, and it was at this juncture, my mother said, that this man who'd paid faint attention to spiritual matters apparently had his epiphany, recognized his mortality, and professed his faith in the Lord Jesus. I pray that's the case, that I might see my earthly father again in eternity.

Following this emergency—which proved to be stark foreshadowing—Reva and I sat in the hospital's parking lot the morning we drove back to California. I wanted to see Dad again before we left, but Reva dissuaded me, saying it would be too stressful for either of us. She was right.

In California, Reva and I rented a mobile home. To describe it as decrepit would be a wild euphemism. It was old and beaten up and tiny—and heated in the evenings by a kerosene stove which Reva almost had to stand on her head to light. (I refused to go near it, macho as I was. I didn't fear death, but I wasn't about to summon it with a match…) When her folks flew cross-country to visit, we suggested—emphatically suggested—they stay at a nearby hotel, where accommodations would be up to their standards. No way. Our "place" would be "just fine," they insisted. Now Harry Pickitt was, without fail, one of the most courteous men I've ever met, always smiling, always encouraging, always a glass-half-full kind of guy. But that night in our mobile home, I heard him groan as he sat down on that creaking bed, which surely tested his benevolent spirit. Just before they returned to Michigan, Harry handed us a gasoline credit card. "Oh, I want to give you this," he said, in an off-handed sort of way. "Besides, it's about to expire." The card, of course, was nowhere near its expiration. From that point on, armed with car and card, Reva and I became instant heroes among our California friends as we could travel, picnic and sightsee without crimping our meager budget. The gift was vintage Harry: he was always there to help without making me feel uncomfortable.

In addition to working on heavy equipment—bulldozers, trucks, cranes and drilling equipment—I was also placed in charge of training the rest of my company on a Bucyrus-Erie "spudder" after the instructor came to understand how my oilfield experience had left me better versed than he (or anyone else on base) in the operation and idiosyncrasies of that piece of machinery. When I completed Seabee training, the Navy gave me a choice of duty stations, and I picked Guam. Gene, Betty and Janis came to see me before I shipped out, and Reva returned to Michigan with them.

After the Korean War ended in July, 1953, we were essentially killing time there on Guam, playing baseball and preparing for football, when in September I received a tough message: my father had died. How clearly I remember. It was a Wednesday (called *rope-yarn Sunday* meaning an extra day when the athletic fields and the offices were closed and only emergency business was conducted).

When I got word about Dad's passing, I walked up to the office area where a lieutenant commander spotted me and said, "John, "I'm sorry about your dad. Why aren't you packing to go home?"

"There's no one here to make that possible today," I said.

"You go call your family. Tell them you're on the way. Take my Jeep to the airport. I'll pick up your luggage and meet you there."

By the time I reached the airstrip, an officer was standing ready with my necessary orders. He walked me to the plane. These orders transferred me back to Great Lakes Naval Station for immediate discharge. Meanwhile, the lieutenant commander had arrived with my bags (remember, I was only a petty officer) and personally carried them onto the plane, a gesture that prompted a lot of incredulous stares and questions from other military personnel sharing my flight.

After a few days in Michigan, I proceeded to the Great Lakes Naval Station (where I'd done boot camp) according to the orders for discharge. But there was a glitch. The officer reading (and interpreting) my paperwork insisted I first had to serve out the prescribed duration of my duty time. My new assignment: driving a bus around the grounds. I felt disheartened, but bit my tongue.

About a week later I encountered the same officer, who blurted, "What are YOU doing here?"

I motioned toward my vehicle. "Sir, I'm driving this bus, as assigned."

He said, "I mean what are you doing HERE? I followed up on your orders by contacting the main office in Guam. Their response was crystal clear: 'to proceed with discharge.' I thought you were already out of here. As of right now—this moment—you are discharged!"

Here again is proof of the muscle of faith. My family needed me home at a time when official protocol made that appear impossible. But once again, the Lord had interceded and provided the means in answer to my prayers.

OUR MICHIGAN OIL BUSINESS BEGINNING

"A good name is rather to be chosen than great riches, and loving favour rather than silver and gold." (Proverbs 22:1)

MILLER BROTHERS PARTNERSHIP

It was 1953. Dad was gone. We buried him in the Allegan Oakwood Cemetery just a couple of miles from home. His business was no more…with the exception of a storage yard and some drilling equipment—three rigs, three trucks and trailers. Little money. No debt. It now fell to us boys—Gene, Jack and me—to determine how to negotiate the slippery slopes of family business and family finances. Tough terrain, for while we had all worked in the oilfield, none of us was especially enthralled with the notion of making it a career.

My knee-jerk instinct was to sell everything and return to my plan of entering the sand and gravel business with my father-in-law. There we were, with the Michigan oil and gas exploration industry in decline, with so many proven fields all drilled up.[6]

There was no choice. It was either use the equipment or lose it to rust and neglect. Brother Gene and I were the oldest, he at 23, I at 22, and had worked with Dad in the business in some measure since we were twelve. Brother Jack, younger and with newly

---

[6] At the time there were forty-two Michigan Lower Peninsula counties with proven oil or gas production and the number of holes drilled per year was hovering in the mid-300s and would decline to as few as 207 before beginning the next upturn in 1958.

pregnant Phyllis, was driving truck and living under the lengthening shadow of the military draft.

Gene and I[7] formed the Miller Brothers partnership in early 1954, beginning as a drilling company taking nearby jobs for a day rate. (Benevolent father-in-law Harry loaned us $10,000 to jumpstart the business.) Jack stepped aside since right then he thought he was about to be called up for military service. A short time later he received official word he would remain a civilian, so he promptly became an employee of the newly minted Miller Brothers.

To get work in those days, most drilling contractors would take an interest in the deal. We would negotiate a cash per foot contract and a percentage of interest to drill—lease the land, raise the money, and drill the prospect. Eventually we would also move into oil production.

Over the years, Gene, Jack and I spent uncountable days together and through them all remained very good "friends"—way beyond the DNA that connects us. We three meshed extremely well—not only in business, but recreationally also—all the softball and basketball games, summers in Ludington, short vacations in Florida, etc.

A short time ago, someone asked, "What was the most successful thing you ever did in your business?" I started to recall some of the exceptional wells we had discovered and the huge achievements of our international company, GLOBEX. Then it struck me with absolute, irrefutable clarity: my greatest success—let me say, *blessing*—in business, without question, was how Gene, Jack and I worked together our entire adult lives. We did not work for anyone else; we worked together. Three brothers…together.

Of course, succeeding in business is a wonderful feeling. But succeeding in business with family goes beyond simple words. Not only do you know and respect the executive hierarchy, but you know where you came from having shared all those experiences, down to wrestling in the attic and playing basketball in the driveway, something deep and abiding within your bones, knowing you're a part of each other. What that translated into for us in business was to make each gain doubly sweet and to render each setback far less lonely.

---

[7] I felt any two of us brothers could make it but three together might have friction.

Don't misunderstand me: we had our honest differences. But we could sit down and talk those through without becoming so angry it caused problems. Were we contentious from time to time? Absolutely. We were Millers.

On occasion, we might have retreated home at night and tried to drop-kick the dog out of frustration. But there was never anything that came between Gene, Jack, and me to preclude a discussion of the issues. Most typically we each had a singular passion for a particular phase of the business and therein resided no conflict.

Frankly, I most liked the upfront part of our business—putting deals together, raising money, managing relations with other companies, traveling and getting involved in the political side of our industry.

Gene had the opposite temperament—informed by far different proclivities. He would not have touched the tasks I relished with a ten-foot pole. In fact from 1976 to 1977 Gene served as president of the Michigan Oil And Gas Association (MOGA), a position he liked far better than its duties. He categorically abhorred being behind the podium, making announcements, preparing the agenda for a meeting. At the end of a business meal, he would be scheduled first to address the audience. Invariably, he'd resort to a painful delaying tactic. He would rise quickly, leave the head table and slide out the door into the temporary freedom of a hallway. Then, I presume, he'd hustle into the bathroom to relieve himself or to throw-up … maybe both. In time, he would return to the podium and bang the gavel, calling the meeting to order. Once up front and speaking, he got along in decent shape. It was, however, the sort of responsibility he enjoyed doing not one iota, but he executed it because it was part of the job description. It was a hallmark of Gene as a man—he always did a good job.

Jack, on the other hand, was a strong synthesis of Gene and me, and excelled at running down and gathering all of the details for our land department. On issues related to acreage acquisition, everything funneled back to him. Jack mixed well with people, and that ability came to the fore when he served as president of MOGA in 1988 and 1989. What a trio we made…the Miller brothers in working partnership.

Although the fledgling Miller Brothers was not active in the play that turned the state around in the mid-1950s, the discovery of the Albion-Scipio Trend[8] had a tremendous impact on us. We didn't range too far from Allegan in those days, generally staying within a sixty-mile radius. We were operating up around Scottville, Michigan, near Ludington, and I headed down to the Albion-Scipio area and took some leases near Albion. We hired Don Scott to drill a hole for us, which came up dry. Later we also took farm-outs[9] on a couple of what turned out to be dry holes in southeastern Michigan.

---

[8] Appendix C - Albion-Scipio Trend Discovery in Mid-1950s
[9] Lease owner sells mineral right lease at a reduced interest to receiver.

While Miller Brothers was busily developing Riverton and Scottville, my Uncle George and Lester Harris were returning to their roots to make history again. The headline "New Method Brings in Oil Well in Bloomingdale Field," ran in the Sunday, August 7, 1960 edition of *The Kalamazoo Gazette*. George and Lester had brought in a well that week using a relatively new technique called sand fracing (fracing being the abbreviation for fracturing). The process "employs water, sand and acid to crack hard rock formations holding trapped deposits of oil and gas in the Traverse Geological Formation…" the news story explained.

Lester Harris, Gene Evans, and Uncle George bring in the new Bloomingdale well - August, 1960

Uncle George was quoted as saying, "Fracing was developed about 1956 and while it might not be perfect, we've proved that it works…" Today sand fracs are an everyday oilfield occurrence, but it's neat to know how another member of the Miller family was at the cutting edge of oil production enhancement technology, even though George's operations had separated from Dad's years before.

LUDINGTON:
A TURNING POINT FOR MILLER BROTHERS

We had managed to find a little oil at three places by 1958 and had an opportunity to take a farm-out from Superior Oil Company in Riverton Township, Mason County, Michigan. To get this deal consummated, we had to fly down to Houston to meet with Bob Newcomb, a Michigan petroleum exploration legend, a man highly regarded as a classical geologist and reputed to be extremely bright.

We knew little about Houston. It was the first time we had ever taken a business trip when we flew out to meet with Newcomb, had the discussion, and made the deal to farm-in the acreage so we could drill in that area. We bored the hole late in 1957 and hit pay dirt early in 1958—our first discovery—then moved into production. It was not a large find (fifteen barrels a day) but it got us jump-started, and we were exhilarated just to have that initial taste of success.

1958 - First discovery of the year - Riverton Township, Mason County - me with Gene, Jim Walker, and Lee Cook

Back in Allegan one day, I dropped by Mother's house. She asked how things were going, and I explained about the well and how pleased we were. I told her we had enough acreage to drill at least ten to fifteen holes there, which translated into the possibility of 150-200 barrels a day.

She looked at me awhile and asked why we limited it to "fifteen barrels per well per day."

"Well, that's just based on what we got in the first well."

She said, "Don't you think God is able to provide something larger than that?"

Her comment challenged me. Why was I not thinking in bigger numbers?

Bottom line: the next well we drilled and completed flowed over 300 barrels a day. Needless to add, we fell in love with Mason County's potential, which explains why that area around Scottville became our home-away-from-home for a decade as it blessed us beyond our expectations. That second well was very strong and triggered our development of the Riverton Field, which grew into eighteen producing wells as Miller Brothers ended up with essentially all the productive acreage in the field. So Riverton proved a catapult for us as we maintained our contracting work and simultaneously started taking on more deals in which we acquired the acreage or worked with private geologists, first scouting out sites to drill and then producing the wells ourselves.

About this time we met a gifted geologist from Mt. Pleasant named Bill Brown, who was working north of the Riverton Field. Brown knew the Michigan oil patch intimately, and his geology was as flawless as his integrity. We had developed acreage in the Riverton 12 reservoir, with fifteen completed wells in the area. At the time we drilled our first

Our Mason County "field office" in 1962 — John Wirth, Jack and me

well in Riverton and finished that project, Bill was working farther north, by Scottville, so we acquired all of that acreage and drilled there as well.

That area, too, was extremely productive and awfully good to us, and while we were there, we started looking at older fields in the area, conceivably to purchase from major oil companies. We ended up buying the Sippy Property south and east of Scottville, which had previously been a strong producing field owned by Superior Oil Company. We negotiated a deal to buy that property, which in turn gave us a place to store equipment in a remote location. We produced those wells and set up our shop, where we maintained our mechanical and welding facility. We also provided a place for people to stay, a cabin with indoor plumbing, some bedrooms and living space. It worked out fine for our operations. Shortly thereafter, we negotiated and bought the Stony Lake Field and the Pentwater Field from Exxon, successor to Carter Oil.

When we had drilled the first well in Riverton, we moved a rig in just about deer season, around mid-November. The weather was starting to worsen, somewhat snowy, and we brought in a trailer previously used for deer hunting. Naturally it had no indoor toilet, but afforded us a place to sleep out of the weather and in proximity to the rig site.

That's the way our drilling operation worked back then, edging toward the primitive. There was an outhouse which migrant workers used during summer stays in Michigan, and it wasn't too far from our trailer. We also carried in our own water for drinking and for washing. It finally got to snowing so thick we couldn't see enough to get out of the driveway to head for the main road without tying a flag on the antenna in order to alert oncoming traffic. It was a challenging way to live, but you did what you needed to make the whole thing go.

To operate the drilling rig, we worked on a pair of twelve-hour shifts—one of us noon to midnight, the other midnight to noon. Sometimes Gene, Jack and I would all be on one job; other times we'd be scattered over different sites. It all hinged on the immediate needs.

We hired personnel who knew the oil and gas business, the best people we could find, and most stayed with us many years. We tried to treat our employees like extended family, giving them as much work as we could and distributing bonuses when our business prospered.

The work was hard, uncompromising. We would leave Allegan between 3 and 5 a.m. on Monday morning to be in Scottville by daylight. We would then try to leave Saturday afternoon so we could have some time with our families.

By God's grace, Reva was a rock. During those years she played dual roles of Mom-and-Dad during the week, raising and disciplining our growing quartet who ranged in age from five to ten. Her stoic assessment of this challenging period? "That's-just-the-way-it-was."

Me with Boone Cook (right) alongside my car, stuck at well location

It was a tough, grinding operation, and we did that for four years before things broke over to where we could have a more conventional work environment and a more sane schedule. At the same critical time it was Reva, Betty and Phyllis—the dynamic triumvirate—who glued everything together on the home-front while we men were away. The ladies were the heroes.

GREAT PEOPLE
WE'VE MET IN THE MICHIGAN OIL BUSINESS

I would be remiss in this memoir if I failed to chronicle and profile some of the extraordinary individuals I met along the way—folks who imprinted and shaped the industry that was my lifeblood.

WILLIAM F. (BILL) BROWN

A gentle, soft-spoken man who chose his words after thoughtful contemplation, Bill was born in Iron Mountain, Michigan, the land of hard-rock geology, in 1903, and graduated from the University of Michigan in 1925, the same year as the Saginaw Oilfield discovery that put Michigan into the commercially producing oil industry. After laboring for the state of Michigan in its geological survey division, Brown worked for Pure Oil (discoverers of the Mt. Pleasant Oil Field in 1928), then for Cities Service before becoming an independent geologist under the name of Mountain Oil and Gas, which he operated until his death in December 1989. Brown was expert in both the regulatory and the private sectors of the business. A good friend of Miller Brothers, Bill was integral to getting us involved in the fledgling Niagaran Pinnacle Reef play. On a personal level, we enjoyed spending time with Bill and his wife, Alice, and at times we would enjoy a hunting trip to South Dakota.

Bill Brown, me and E. Allan Morrow at a 1971 MOGA meeting.

E. ALLAN MORROW
Allan Morrow, a transplant from Tennessee, had come to Michigan to work for Walter McClanahan. Allan was born in Adairsville, Kentucky, graduated from Furman

University in Greenville, South Carolina, and started working for McClanahan in Michigan in 1933 as a geological clerk. In 1934, he returned to Murfreesboro, Tennessee, to marry Bernice, a gracious woman and steadfast helpmate.

Following McClanahan's fatal heart attack in 1940 on the golf course at Sea Island, Georgia, and following Roosevelt Oil Company's subsequent acquisition of McClanahan's Midwest Refinery, Allan returned to Mt. Pleasant. In 1954 he became president of Roosevelt Oil and Refining Corp., and when Roosevelt merged with Leonard Refineries and Midwest Refineries, the company named him director and vice president. Allan was an extraordinary gentleman, liked by everybody. In fact, people used to comment, not facetiously, that it was almost better to be turned down by Allan than be accepted by somebody else, because just talking with Allan made you feel so good.

He was also zealous in civic affairs, serving as chairman of the Isabella Bank and Trust Board of Directors, as president of the Mt. Pleasant Chamber of Commerce, president of the Central Michigan University Board of Governors, and president of MOGA from 1957-1958. He also contributed unstintingly to the building and operations of Central Michigan Community Hospital.

Allan was a straight-up guy, a solid friend, and dependable business associate. He passed in 1998, a year after he had lost Bernice following sixty-three years of exemplary marriage.

VANCE ORR SR.

Originally from Tennessee, Vance Orr Sr. had come to Michigan in 1935 to work for his uncle, Walter McClanahan, a legendary Michigan oilfield pioneer. McClanahan was a promoter who made it big with the Struble No. 1 well in Section 15 of Greendale Township, Midland County in 1931. Among McClanahan's personnel imports to the Michigan oil business were E. Allan Morrow, and his nephew Vance Orr Sr., a gentleman and "good 'ol boy" with roots two-decades deep in the Michigan oil fraternity.

E. Allan Morrow and Vance Orr Sr. in 1946. Neither of them ever explained what the occasion was that made Allan doze off, or why Orr had his eye bandaged.

I remember clearly my first meeting with Vance. He was a geologist then with McClure Oil in Alma, Michigan. While his company was securing a lot of drilling contracts, they had begun phasing out their rigs, and Miller Brothers wanted to get in line to do some of that business. In those early days it was a rare occasion when I dressed in clean clothes for work, yet there I was one morning—all spit and polish—driving to Mt. Pleasant with Reva beside me, to confer with Vance. While I attended the meeting in the McClure offices, she stayed patiently in the car. Vance and I chatted until almost noon. Just as I was thinking that Reva was no doubt dead-tired of sitting there, waiting and waiting, Vance offered to take me to lunch.

I hesitated. "Well, my wife is in the car."

Vance flashed me an impish grin and quipped, "She knows how to eat, doesn't she?" That lay the foundation for a tight friendship that lasted until he died in 2004, in his 90s.

Vance was a wonderful man—an outstanding, honest, kind, and helpful person along with his wife Emily. In addition to being a great friend who shared many of my spiritual beliefs and family values, he served as president of MOGA from 1992-1993 and in a number of lesser capacities, most notably on the public relations committee of IPAA. A key player in a multi-generational business, he became known as *Senior* when his son Vance (Pinky) Orr *Junior* joined the ranks of the Michigan oil and gas industry.

HAROLD M. McCLURE JR.

Harold was a genuine, gung-ho-go-get-'em guy who was already flying airplanes when the rest of us were still looking for a used car. He was flamboyant—never down, always the rah-rah cheerleader, on-fire, electric. He also had a well deserved reputation for being slow-on-the-draw when you were looking for payment following a completed job. So I suspect God dropped Harold into our lives to stretch the Miller Brothers' patience—and no doubt a lot of others' too...

Harold was always thinking several moves down the line, like some fanatical chess player, and on occasion his vision for both his company and our industry would

1967 - At IPAA in Houston, Michigan oilmen congratulate 46-year-old Harold McClure Jr. for being first Michigan president elected to head the organization – Bill Myler, McClure, I. W. "Bucky" Hartman, Fred Turner and me.

overwhelm and derail present exigencies. A talk with Harold was a romp into his infectious enthusiasm for the project or cause du jour. He was like Gene Hackman firing up his basketball team in the movie *Hoosiers*. Just talking to him pumped up your pride in being an oilman.

Harold was third-generation. His grandfather had been an oilman in Ohio and Pennsylvania, and his father, Harold M. McClure Sr., was an indisputable legend in the Michigan patch: prominent oil and gas producer; third president of MOGA; one of the framers of Michigan Act 61; and a member of the first Michigan Oil and Gas Advisory Board created by that act.

Born in 1921, McClure Jr. graduated high school in 1938 at sixteen (like me), and that same year started his own oilfield supply company, Allegan Pipe and Tool. He was ten years my senior and preceded me both as president of MOGA and as president of IPAA. His contributions to the industry were enormous: one of the pioneer developers of Michigan's largest oil field (the Albion-Scipio Trend); MOGA president (beginning a tradition of father-and-son leadership terms in the organization) in 1961-62; first Michigan oilman elected president of IPAA in 1967-68; and driller of the deepest hole ever bored in Michigan in search of oil and gas (17,468 feet near Ithaca in Gratiot County) in 1975-76. It was dry.

His longtime friend, Norman X. Lyon, editor of the Michigan Oil & Gas News from 1929 until his 1991 death at 82, said of Harold M. McClure Jr. following Harold's passing in 1977 at the early age of 56 after a long fight with cancer:

"McClure believed in the young generations but didn't deny the older. His companies often provided the first in-the-field jobs for geology and engineering graduates. In his career, Harold was responsible for, or involved in, many of Michigan's better oil and gas finds. This wasn't by chance or all luck. He worked at it. He had a keen insight. He was intense. He was confident.

"He once called me to ask just how big I thought the Northern Michigan Niagaran Reef Trend was going to be. At the time only three wells had been drilled successfully in what would be the Trend. 'How about 500 million barrels of oil and three trillion cubic feet of natural gas?'

"I could not believe what I was hearing."

(As of December, 2009, the Northern Michigan Niagaran Reef Trend has produced more than 350 million barrels of oil and 2.2 trillion cubic feet of natural gas.)

"He listened to the scientific community and he never shut the door on a driller or promoter who 'had an idea.'

"He liked the indescribable thrill of wildcat oil and gas drilling. He once said 'Yeah, there has to be some economics but hunting down a new discovery is what really counts.' He helped a good many others do just that."

WILLIAM C. MYLER

Another supreme friend is William C. "Bill" Myler, son of the iconic Charles Myler, whose Muskegon Development Company drilled the Muskegon Field discovery well. A host of test wells were drilled from 1925 to 1927 with minimal results and Michigan's days as an oil-producing state might well have been numbered if not for the Muskegon Field. Oil and gas shows had been reported sporadically in Western Michigan wells drilled for salt and ancillary purposes since the turn of the 20th century, so Muskegon County was prime petroleum-prospecting territory.

Intrigued by the oil and gas industry, brothers-in-law Charles Myler, an accountant, and Stanley Daniloff, a tailor, formed Muskegon Oil Corporation (today Muskegon Development Company), raised capital, and drilled their first well in July of 1926—a find that reported light oil shows and was encouraging enough for investors to approve a second try.

A Standard Oil of Indiana subsidiary, Dixie Oil Company was also active in that same area adjacent to Muskegon Oil Company lease holdings, and Dixie's geologist Hugh D. Crider was especially anxious for a proven well there to justify the leases his company had taken. Crider advised Myler-Daniloff and their investors to drill at a location four miles north of Muskegon in an area already subdivided for industrial and residential use.

On December 8, 1927, the Reeths #1 encountered natural gas in the Traverse Formation at 1,640 feet. Drilling continued to 1,700 feet where oil was encountered. The well's flow reached a rate of 330 barrels per day, then settled in at about fifty. That Muskegon discovery, blessed with a prime location near a center with shipping infrastructure by both land and water, elicited eager responses from major oil companies and from independents across the state and around the nation. The boom intensified when Dixie successfully drilled a second well on 200 acres it had acquired in its arrangement with Muskegon Oil, and then Muskegon Oil bored another well. Expanding its holdings to more than 50,000 acres as fast as leases could be written, Muskegon Oil organized Muskegon Development Company with three subsidiaries—Citizens Petroleum, Lakeshore Petroleum and Juliet-Morris Development Company.

Bill Myler was born in 1925, the same year the Saginaw Field validated and established Michigan in the oil business. So Bill was just a toddler when his dad made that historic Muskegon Field discovery.

We have had a number of fine associates in Michigan, but Bill's has been one of our deepest and longest friendships, and he has participated with us in myriad deals. In 1965, when Bill and I were both under consideration for presidency of MOGA, he stepped aside in order to straighten out a few pressing business matters, which afforded me the opportunity to assume office. Later he would succeed me in that position.

Vance Orr Sr., Gene, me, and Bill Myler in 1968 at the Peacock Field

Bill owned some leases in the Lake County area, where there had been a new discovery called the Peacock Field and Miller Brothers also had acreage there. Chatting over lunch one day, we decided to trade interests in each other's acreage. One of us laid out what we instantly agreed to: "We'll take a piece of yours; you take a piece of ours, and we'll drill a well." Whose words? I'd prefer to think the suggestion was mine… Bill's acreage proved to be the "barn burner," way beyond our wildest hopes, almost too good for any initial joint venture.

In preparation for the state lease sale for developing the Northern Niagaran Reef Trend—an area that covered seven Michigan counties—I worked late into the night assembling pertinent materials, then arrived early in Lansing before the sale started, while Bill and Gene remained up at the Peacock well site, preparing to drill in.

I was summoned out of the sale to take a phone call from Gene. Along with the daily drilling report, he advised that they would run pipe because the formation seemed to be running high and looking good. Having checked it out, Bill and Gene said they would prepare the pipe for subsequent drill-in. I agreed and returned to the sale.

Later that morning another call came from Gene, this one with pressing urgency, and I could hear a pounding, rushing sound in the background, which I couldn't identify. I raised my voice and, cupping the phone, asked what in the world was going on. Gene shouted that they had planned to run the pipe and cement it, but then questioned their accuracy. So they drilled into the top of the pay and ended up deepening the hole a little.

Still I couldn't identify that deafening, whooshing noise and demanded to know what it was. Gene yelled, "It's the well flowing out of control!"

Finally everything calmed down enough for me to return to the meeting. I had just recently become a member of the Michigan Oil and Gas Advisory Board, whose function was to assist in problem-solving for the industry. When I walked into the meeting that morning following Gene's exuberant phone call, the first comment out of the state guy's mouth was: "Miller's got a well up there that's leaking barrels, and their equipment isn't holding up very good!" My buddies rode me plenty hard all that day.

Understanding the press of the situation, I rushed to the well site where Bill, Gene and I finally shut down the super-charged leak. At that point, we began running pipe into the hole to prepare it for production when all of a sudden…I don't know what caused it…but some pent-up pressure blew the plugs right out of the pipe, and that well jetted 60 feet high—just going wild and crazy.

Gene and I knew someone had to get in there to unscrew that pipe and get a nipple set up with a valve, or we would soon be in far more dire straits. The question was: who would that someone be?

George Jenks, a courageous guy who had been working with us for some time, agreed to assist me in attacking the crisis. First we had to build a scaffold ("once a Seabee …") in order to climb up off the rig floor to access and unscrew the problematic joint of tubing. Gene was on the platform, holding tight to the rope we tied around the tubing—to prevent it from blowing over and hitting the metal mast connected to the metal pipe, which could set off a spark that would incinerate us all—while George and I frantically worked to unscrew the joint. (Bill watched from a safe distance.) With the valve wide open, we jammed it into place (it would have blown right up out of our hands if it had been closed), screwed it into the top of the tubing, and then started tightening it by hand. When we finally clenched it all the way down, we could at last shut off the well and subdue its dark fury.

When we finished, there was oil lacquering the rig and everything within a 100-yard radius—soaking me, George, and Gene. (But not Bill.) Everything within sight lay coated in black shimmery crude with its iridescent green cast. That blow-out resulted in one of the biggest messes Miller Brothers ever encountered. In the end, we were so relieved to get it under control without further complications and without a mob of official people converging on us to tell us what to do—and so thankful nobody was injured in the process. Need I state the obvious? We had hit an exceptional well.

The Miller/Myler partnership ended up drilling a total of six wells in Peacock, with the original one, in all its wildness, the best by far. Thus commenced our singular business relationship with Bill Myler and Muskegon Development.

In the 1960s, with Bill at its helm, Muskegon Development moved from Muskegon to Mt. Pleasant, Michigan, where Bill and his son, William (Billy) C. Myler Jr., continue to manage the company's large oil and gas interests. Both Mylers have served as chief elected leaders of MOGA: Bill Sr. as president 1968-1969 and Bill Jr. as chairman of the board 1998-1999. Together the Miller and Myler families have supplied MOGA with six elected chiefs.

To this day we still collaborate in business ventures and still enjoy unparalleled

Mike, me, Bill Myler, and Bill Myler, Jr., all former Michigan Oil And Gas Association elected leaders, at a recent golf outing

friendship with the Myler family. Our sons—Bill Jr., Mike, and Kelly—who comprise our third generation, are all roughly the same age and continue in that dual tradition of friendship and business, exemplifying the collegiality and integrity that ensue when folks in a superlative industry share opportunity and vision and faith.

RICHARD (DICK) L. BURGESS

Originally hailing from Canada, Dick Burgess is another great friend in the Michigan oil industry whose background was geology. Dick was the former president of Northern Michigan Exploration Company and 1983-84 Michigan Oil And Gas Association president. He proved himself over many years to be an ultra-dependable friend and a genuine industry leader.

G.R. (ROLLIE) DENISON

Rollie Denison was a young coach at the Allegan High School during my youth. He had an accounting degree and would later get involved with the oil industry in Mt. Pleasant, becoming president of Lease Management (Michigan's premier independent oilfield service company); becoming president of MOGA (1970-71); and, with his wife Olga, becoming one of Central Michigan University's most generous alumni as well as a community leader.

MY INVOLVEMENT WITH MOGA

Vance Orr Sr. was instrumental in getting me invited to a Michigan Oil And Gas Association Board meeting. Miller Brothers' success with the Riverton Field had earned us attention as producers/operators and elevated us beyond the ranks of drillers-for-hire. After attending a few meetings, I was asked to consider joining the MOGA Board. Realizing fully how this membership would benefit our company, I agreed and was elected to a two-year board term beginning January 1, 1961 and ending December 31, 1962.

In October, 1965, I was elected the 20th president of MOGA beginning in January 1966. At the age of 34, I was the youngest person ever to hold that position. In October 1966, I was re-elected to serve another one-year term as president in 1967. My becoming president of MOGA increased Miller Brothers' recognition throughout the state and afforded me opportunities to mingle and work with the presumptive movers and shakers of our industry. Most critically, this affiliation boosted our profile and enhanced our networking, raised the quality of our operations, and gave us entrée to bigger, better deals.

Back then Mount Pleasant was the indisputable center of the Michigan oil business, and if your company wasn't based there, you were outside the circle of the in-group, which meant you had virtually no chance of ever being considered for the presidency of MOGA. Despite my ostensible lack of credentials, MOGA members and board apparently recognized something in me that I couldn't envision at the time and elected me president. I only knew a few of that sanctified in-group personally through our operations, and indeed there were some among the oldest, grayest beards who didn't want my presidency to happen.

At the time, Michigan producers were being paid a depressed price for crude oil at the wellhead relative to what it was fetching in other states. Far worse, it was a static price that hadn't changed in twenty years, even while business expenses had risen substantially. The price/cost squeeze spun our industry into crisis until our biggest challenge became just staying alive in the business. By then some of us were close to needing life-support.

Michigan producers had few options, save to sell our crude at the prevailing state price of $2.85 to $2.90 per barrel. The ready availability of Canadian oil exerted even more pressure on us, and we knew too well that if we didn't acquiesce to the going price structure, purchasers would simply import more from across the border. So there we were, locked into economic suicide: we were virtually producing ourselves out of business. Adversity has a way of rallying people with common goals and common problems for their collective survival. To that end, one of my achievements as MOGA president was to encourage greater participation by our members in regularly scheduled

(continued on page 67)

C. JOHN MILLER
PHOTO ALBUM

Reva and me with first-born, Mike, at 8 months old in 1955.

Reva, me, Betty.

Mother and me.

Above:
Reva and me

Left:
Gene and me relaxing.

Right:
Gene and me in 2010

61

Jack, Mother, me, Joan, Janis, and Gene in 1978

Mike, Sara, Sally, me, Reva and Cindy,
1974 IPAA Convention San Francisco

Back Row: Cindy, Mike and Sally. Front Row: Sara, Reva, me about 1972

Mike, Cindy, Reva, me, Sally and Sara
Gull Lake – August 2010

Me, Pat Jones, Reva and A. V. Jones Jr.

John and Diane Jones with Reva and me on the golf course

Tom & Carol Harding, me, John & Sharon Garside, Reva, Pat & A. V. Jones, Jr.

With trusted friend and IPAA colleague Joe Farmer

Receiving the Chief Roughneck Award at the October 1975 IPAA Annual Meeting in Dallas, Texas.

With Harold M. McClure Jr., former Texas Governor John Connally, and A. V. Jones Jr. at the 1976 New Orleans IPAA meeting.
(Note that I have my eyes closed, a Miller family trait that has plagued me for decades. Reva was constantly at war with photographers for taking pictures that made me look tipsy, when I don't even drink.

(continued from page 60)
meetings. When I assumed office, policy was to invite only directors to monthly gatherings, all the time questioning why we couldn't build stronger membership involvement throughout the state.

So the first idea I implemented was to invite anybody and everybody in membership to attend meetings and to provide through that format a variety of informative programs addressing prospective industry issues, all presented by sharp speakers with expertise. It wasn't long before we were getting 150-200 people at the monthly gatherings rather than the normal 30. That double focus upon inclusiveness and education proved unique across the country, and as a result, MOGA leadership received national recognition for our innovation and foresight. Of course, when you start having younger folks attend, many of the staid, gainsaying older guard did not know three quarters of the room…

Helping with my official duties as MOGA President (testing the hot dogs at the 1966 MOGA Picnic), were Joe Molley, Gene Miller, and Bill Myler

The second change I initiated was to introduce every person present by name, with an amplifying comment to recognize and affirm each participant. That technique sailed well too as MOGA became the only association in the United States holding a monthly meeting with such enthusiastic attendance.

During 1966 and 1967, 835 Michigan drilling permits were issued, resulting in 824 holes being drilled, yielding 125 oil wells, 38 natural gas wells, and 577 dry holes. Michigan crude oil prices averaged $2.87 per barrel while natural gas wellhead prices averaged between 58 cents and 64 cents per thousand cubic feet.

The December 23, 1966 issue of The Michigan Oil & Gas News printed my first summation to the MOGA membership:

"The year 1966 has been a challenge for each and every one of us associated in the oil and gas industry. We have been beset by continually rising costs in all phases of our activities, plagued by a continual shortage of competent labor and, most importantly, have continued to dispose of our great commodity at a price inconsistent with the time and conditions in which we live.

"In spite of these mounting problems, a healthy spirit has been maintained in the Michigan industry. New fields of production have been opened and a steady, though less than desirable, rate of exploratory activity has continued.

"The word most often heard to offer a cure-all for our ills has been INCENTIVE. This word, INCENTIVE, is normally directed at thoughts of political, economic, and other factors of direct operation.

"I would like to suggest that while we recognize the necessity of continued research to correct the obvious areas of concern, we do have a great deal of INCENTIVE that may be overlooked. Our INCENTIVES include operating in a state that can use, and in fact needs, additional oil and gas reserves; not being subjected to extreme proration; and operating in warm rapport with a Department of Conservation (later Department of Natural Resources, then Department of Environmental Quality and about to be Department of Natural Resources again) that ranks among the best in the entire nation.

"Further INCENTIVES are the support of a strong Michigan Oil And Gas Association. We have the INCENTIVE of living in a Free Country and enjoying Blessings no other country has ever been privileged to experience.

"In summary, while our problems are complex, our INCENTIVES and opportunities are multifarious, consequently our attitude should be one of optimism and enthusiasm."

Reviewing those words over four decades later, I can see how some of the points may need tweaking to fit today's business climate, but I cannot change the clarion call, and the imperative need, to maintain and emphasize our enthusiasm and optimism.

CHANGES IN DIRECTION FOR MILLER BROTHERS

During the late 1960s, Michigan drilling trended to deeper geological zones with the discovery of Niagaran Pinnacle Reefs (rock-encased remains of ancient coral in which huge quantities of oil and natural gas accumulated) at depths ranging from 5,000 to 7,000 feet in the northern Lower Peninsula of Michigan. For the most part, our drilling equipment was oriented to shallow finds—from 1,500 to 4,000 feet. With deeper drilling came increased pressures, larger casings and greater risks of blowouts, all of which demanded more sophisticated equipment. We didn't want to move into that phase of the drilling/contracting business, so we reduced our involvement in that arena and opted to focus more intently on making and developing deals of our own.

Our partnership, Miller Brothers, was doing very well at this time. Simultaneously, while serving as senior vice-president of Leonard Refinery, my long-time friend Allan Morrow confided that his company wanted to get into the production end of the business, moving in the process beyond just the refining and distribution.

How timely. He offered us the opportunity to manage the geology, land acquisition, and drilling operations for his company while Leonard Refinery would become a silent partner. Their terms: we would receive twenty-five percent of the deal, plus coverage of our business expenses.

Because Leonard and a contingent of other refineries had mistreated and abused Michigan petroleum producers in the past (remember that contemptible squeeze I referenced), we held some grudges. Still, that situation had never dirtied Allan Morrow. Besides, I liked him a great deal—his honesty and cordiality, his deep, smooth professionalism.

Gene and I talked for three hours one afternoon as we drove from Allegan to St. Clair, Michigan, discussing all aspects of the deal, determined at first to just say "No." Then we both did a reverse pivot and decided to try it, which proved in hindsight an excellent call as we ended up being active participants in a superb oil and gas play. In addition to the property we developed with Leonard Refinery, we also had extensive ownership in exploration activity on our own acquired acreage.

Of course, not all good things result from systematic planning and pursuit. There's also serendipity. Early 1971 I was in Scottville, Michigan, in Mason County, having lunch one day with Allan Morrow and Bill Brown when I received a message from the home office saying I needed to call a number which I did not recognize. My secretary noted it was critical. I ended up contacting Doug Lott, a former employee of Miller Brothers whom we had hired to assist in the Scottville field. Though totally new to the drilling business, Doug was very smart—and a quick learner. (In addition, he was a strong athlete, so we had great softball games while working in the Scottville area. Softball, in fact, became our summer pastime during the four or five evenings we would be there – Emery, Gene, Jack, Doug, Les Hansen, Jackie Lawber, and myself, et al.)

After leaving our firm, Doug had taken his degree in accounting, then moved to Gaylord and was now working for a realtor there named Bud Gottloeb. Doug's call that morning was in reference to a piece of land in the Gaylord area owned by Gottloeb.

Shell Oil had drilled a producing well near this parcel and approached Gottloeb about leasing his property. Doug and his boss were offering, instead, to lease the land to Miller Brothers if we would match the Shell number. When I heard the price—$30,000 for a 100-acre lease—I just about dropped the phone. Our typical offer ranged from $5-$20 per acre.

"Doug, how much time do I have to decide?" I asked.

"Thirty minutes," he said.

I returned to the table, where Bill and Allan immediately quizzed me. I relayed the information, and they asked what my response was going to be. I had been praying continually since Doug's call, and within ten minutes these two friends volunteered to ante up $5,000 apiece. We debated awhile, then I returned Doug's call and promised I would have the money for him and Gottloeb the next day.

Meanwhile, both Bill and Allan wondered what Gene's response would be to the morning's impulsive transaction, so we piled into the car and headed over to Ludington where he was having lunch. Allan and Bill were especially anxious to watch Gene's face when he heard about our newest deal.

Gene was just finishing when we arrived, and he asked how we three all happened to be together—and had something happened. As I delineated the terms, my brother never smiled, never scowled, never showed any change of expression whatsoever, just wore that mask of the master poker player.

Finally, Allan could take the silence no longer. "Gene, what are you thinking?" he blurted.

Gene's answer was classic: "I'm going to have some pie…would you like to join me?"

We couldn't stop laughing for an hour. That response epitomized the type of partnership, friendship, and brotherhood Gene and I shared.

(In the end, we didn't have to accept any money from Allan and Bill, but we did include them in the Gaylord well at a reduced cost and added them into some later deals in the Mason-Ludington area. By then, Allan had retired, and he informed us that he was doing better financially in retirement than when he was working.)

We did not have the $30,000 on hand and in cash, and we generally disdained borrowing, but in this case we decided to try it. I called a banker friend in Grand Rapids, explaining our need, and he told me to come by in the morning on my way to Gaylord, that everything would be ready. We never were good customers of any bank because we so abhorred debt. However, we started a long-term relationship with Michigan National that day, and I even served on their board for a number of years.

The deal grew in complexity. As part of the Gottloeb lease acquisition, we needed some title curative work. My job was to sell working interests in the project while Gene handled the drilling and production. During the title search, Jack determined that Shell acreage covered 1/30th of the Gottloeb property.

I knew the Shell executives well, so I called their Denver office and discussed the matter with T. Tommy Thompson, their land manager. He indicated that if the acreage had been any good, Shell would have already acquired the lease. I didn't appreciate his comment, but simply responded that we could give his company an override.

Tommy answered, "Too small to fool with; we'll give it to you." And Shell did.

We had a number of additional problems, re' title work, to clear up before we could drill our first well on this acreage, and during this time, Shell completed theirs on the adjacent property, which turned out to be a strong oil and gas producer.

We drilled the Gaylord-Mortgage #1-16 well in the fall of 1971. We had pre-determined by a combination of scientific geology and seat-of-the-pants guesstimates where certain formations should be, and early indicators proved encouraging. As we were approaching the main indicator, tension mounted and I was on the phone incessantly keeping our investors apprised.

Quite a few people were on hand for the drill-in, the actual penetration of the expected pay zone, called the Niagaran. Bottom line: all of our most aggressive expectations fell far short of what we found. Following drill-in, I drove back to Mt. Pleasant with our geologist, Don Helmboldt, who was frantically scribbling away, calculating and re-calculating all the while.

Finally he stopped and looked over at me, his eyes dancing, and exclaimed, "John, this is a million dollar well!" At this time oil ran around $3.00 per barrel, the highest price we ever had.

We had drilled a few substantial wells before this, but nothing even approaching Don's numbers. We tested the well, and its flow capacity was excellent—500 to 600 barrels of crude per day. We then completed the details for an operating lease, which included a bundle of installations: flow lines from well to tank site, the tanks themselves, and treaters to separate any water from the oil, etc.

A short time later, Gene and Betty traveled to Florida with Reva and me, as the crew at the well-site completed all the connections. While there, we received a call from Bob Acker, Michigan supervisor for oil and gas operations. A good friend, he understood how significant this well was for us. His message was a downer: due to mammoth amounts of natural gas being produced from the oil from the Gaylord-Mortgage #1-16 (and those of other Niagaran producers) huge waste was occurring, so ALL Niagaran wells were being shut-in until gas pipe lines and treating facilities could be erected. Following our early celebration and high exuberance, this announcement was dark with disappointment.

Still, the times proved to be auspicious. Historically, we stood at the starting line of the 1972 oil and gas embargo in the Persian Gulf, when the United States for the first time—save the war years—had to resort to gas rationing. The price of oil shot up meteorically, and here we were, unable to produce or sell ours. It felt like a heavy curse. I questioned in my prayers: Why? We would soon find out.

The U.S. Congress had conceived a dual pricing structure, called Old Oil and New Oil. If a well had been in production prior to May 15, 1973,[10] it was labeled Old Oil and assigned a low, fixed earlier price. But if the well was placed on continuous production after September 30, 1975,[11] it was considered New Oil and would receive the higher market price. The Gaylord-Mortgage #1-16 and all subsequent wells qualified for the higher market price and we ended up selling good amounts of our oil for $20 to $30 a barrel. Additionally, we were able to sell the captured natural gas with a price increase from $.50 to $3.00 per thousand cubic feet (referred to as MCF).

Later we concluded that while Don Helmboldt's math was normally accurate he had made a gargantuan error in his calculation on the Gaylord 1-16: it was not a "million dollar well," it was a "million barrel well" at what was at that juncture the highest per-barrel price in history. It was another of those divine realities that transcended our highest hopes. My assessment: our disappointments are frequently God's appointments.

God's intervention encompassed the following:

- We had no lease, and we had no way to evaluate the prospect's potential except via its proximity to the new Shell well.
- We had to scramble just to get funding.
- We viewed our shut-in at the time as frustration, not blessing.
- In the end, we we sold the natural gas in addition to the oil.

---

[10] Emergency Petroleum Allocation Act of 1973
[11] Energy Policy and Conservation Act of 1975

1975 - Me, Gene, Uncle George and Jack pose in front of the new Miller Brothers office building south of Allegan, Michigan.

In 1975, we opened a modern building just south of Allegan, saying good-bye to the long-standing digs first begun in the basement of my house with a single secretary, then expanded to a small building augmented by an attached mobile home converted into additional space. By now Miller Brothers featured a staff of fifty including the clerical staff, the financial, geophysical and land departments in Allegan and the field employees up north.

Until the mid 1970s, when crude oil prices finally began to climb out of their twenty-five year basement of $3, there was little inducement to lure young folks into our business or to promise them much of a career. Even in our own family, my nineteen-year-old-son Mike had told me he had zero desire in following me into the oil business because at the time he could make more money driving a truck for his Uncle Bill Smith in his sand and gravel operation.

But as prices firmed and as our business gained further traction, we became able to support more family members as employees, and both Mike and Kelly (Gene's son) joined Miller Brothers in 1978 and '79, respectively.

When Mike came on board, I had some early fun with him. I called him into the office and told him, straight-faced and in no uncertain terms, "I just want you to know there is one job around here you can't have."

"What's that?" he asked.

"You can't be loud," I said, recognizing how he had my same Miller tendencies toward high-volume, short-tempered explosions. "Because that is my job—and mine alone. I am the only one who can get excited and start yelling."

With Kelly, it was a similar edict. I said to Kelly, as I stared at him one morning with stony intent, "You, sir, cannot be late. I have already spent half my entire life waiting for your dad. Time after time after time…anywhere from five minutes to an hour, even longer. So, Kelly, I'm telling you up front: Gene has the job of being late for as long as he wants it."

Mike is now president of Miller Energy, and Kelly is president of Eagle Investments. No doubt they've given similar lectures to their sons—the fourth generation coming into our family business. How amazed, how proud, would Clyde be.

The Northern Niagaran Pinnacle Reef Trend continued to bless us, and both our business horizons and our range of acquaintances began to widen exponentially. Gene served as MOGA president in 1976 and again in 1977, just a decade after my tenure, an era when the Niagaran Pinnacle Reef Trend was swinging ahead at full throttle.[12] The seismograph industry had overcome some of the problems caused by the Glacial Drift in reading return signals from below the Dundee Formation in Michigan, thus unlocking the ability to better identify the tall vertical, underlying structures prolific in oil and gas production.

The most significant legislation passed during Gene's MOGA tenure as president involved establishment of the Michigan Natural Resources Trust Fund (MNRTF), created by the Michigan legislature through Public Act 204 in 1976. This fund was the first in the nation to earmark state revenue generated through oil and natural gas industry activities (i.e. state lease sales) for the acquisition or improvement of environmentally sensitive land or for meeting community needs for outdoor recreation.[13]

---

[12] Appendix D - Michigan Oil And Gas Association (MOGA) History & Statistics
[13] Appendix E - Michigan Natural Resources Trust Fund

MILLER BROTHERS OIL CORPORATION

In 1979, Gene and I formed a new business entity—Miller Brothers Oil Corp. (MBOC)—understanding how the early 1980s would necessitate exploration of deeper Michigan geologic zones. Dart Oil Company's discovery of producible natural gas from below 10,000 feet in the Ordovician-age rock (the closest sedimentary "bowl" to the table of bedrock using our "raisin bran" analogy) ushered in a new boom for the Michigan oil and gas exploration industry. There was a shortage of equipment that would drill still deeper, so we invested in a new deep rig to join the hunt for natural gas in the lower geological zones of the state.

If I had to pick a time that the Miller operation turned the corner from an average, medium-sized oil and natural gas producer and began its push toward becoming the worldwide, diversified, private family office we are now under the umbrella of Miller Energy, Inc., it would be the day that Jim Carl joined us in 1980. Only a couple of years out of college, Jim was living in South Bend, Indiana, working as a CPA, all the while itching to get back closer to his roots in Richland, Michigan. At the same time we were looking hard for a controller.

A few months before he interviewed with us, Jim had heard me speak at a Christian Businessmen's Association conference, so from that forum he came to understand the unflinching integrity at the heart of our company. Despite his youth, we hired Jim. And that set huge change into motion for all of us.

Jim's recollection: "At twenty-four, I was the controller of an oil and gas company in the area where I wanted to live. It was a blessing from the Lord. I do think, quite frankly, that when I came onboard, John considered accountants as overhead. I was determined to prove him wrong."

Prove me wrong, he did. In spades.

Back in 1975 we'd started using what was then a state-of-the-art NCR posting machine. Jim immediately persuaded us to move to a mainframe HP computer with an oil-and-gas software package, which would enable us to track our many Niagaran play partnerships. This system proved an invaluable asset and promptly placed us among the first oil and gas operations our size to computerize. In fact, so effective and precise were the accounting systems Jim implemented that we even secured a refund on our Windfall Profits taxes for unprofitable wells.

Jim has always been in the vanguard of higher technology. Long before laptops gained full-blown acceptance in the business community, Jim was banging the pulpit at Miller Energy, insisting we be part of that first wave.

For three decades now, Jim has served as our astute chief financial officer. During that time he has become increasingly savvy about the oilfield, even as I've become more fluent in the language of finance. So it's been the best of symbiotic relationships as we've learned from each other.

But it's Jim who leads us through the nuances of tax code and through the fine print of contracts. We were the first to monetize the Section 29 Unconventional Fuel Tax Credit appropriate to Antrim Shale natural gas production in Michigan, a result of his relentless research. When we sold our producing properties to Conoco in 1984; when we began our Nordhouse Dunes lawsuit; when we took on new partners; when we expanded into other business ventures…when, when, when…it was Jim's intensity and due-diligence and knowledge that led us. Do I sound grateful?

Jim, meanwhile, insists he would never have left public accounting were it not for me, that he sees our relationship as a bond deeper than temporal business. In fact, the scripture he likes to cite is one of my favorites—a spiritual guidepost he and I both live by: *"For everyone to whom much is given, of him shall much be required." (Luke 12:48)*

Miller Energy would not be where we are today—or who we are today—without the thirty years of Jim's financial guidance.

WALKING AMONG THE GIANTS

In the early 1960s, Vance Orr Sr. corralled Reva and me and invited us to attend an Independent Petroleum Association of America (IPAA) meeting in San Francisco with him and his wife, Emily. We had never done anything approaching that. But Vance pressed hard and we agreed to go.

It was heady stuff. There we were, a small drilling-contracting-turned-producing company from a minuscule town in western Michigan rubbing elbows with legends and titans of the independent petroleum industry at a convocation where some of America's key politicians addressed us and visited with us. Here's what amazed me most: they were just people…just ordinary folks. Our problems were similar; our concerns about the industry intersected; and the more we talked with them, the more we discovered how their personal narratives mirrored our own.

In many respects we were at the beginning of a trail a lot of successful independents had already traversed; yet novices that we were, they welcomed us with open arms. Most importantly, I viewed IPAA as a platform where I could promote my convictions and aspirations for the good of both our industry and the nation. It all represented a broader forum for the exchange of ideas, and I looked forward to dialoging with those government officials who could enhance our business climate. A bonus to my entry into the world of IPAA was that there among them, talking and being listened to, was Harold McClure Jr., the guy who used to run the oilfield supply store just down the road when I was a kid in Allegan.

I can't over-emphasize how much I enjoyed the out-front part of the business, and that trip to IPAA opened for me a portal to the world of advocacy on behalf of our industry, a role I'd never dreamed I'd have the opportunity to play. I knew I had found my element and knew I'd been cast upon a broader stage.

I met a number of key people there, including H.A. 'Dave' True Jr. from Casper, Wyoming, who was on his way to becoming president of IPAA in 1962 and again in 1963. Dave had built a ten-company empire from a one-rig drilling outfit and had earned his stripes in agriculture, banking and business, as well as in the oil and gas industry. A brilliant man, he became a self-taught expert in virtually everything he focused on because he studied so diligently to understand structure and detail.

The True Companies started in 1948 when Dave moved from Cody to Casper as manager and part-owner of the one-rig Reserve Drilling Company, a firm that averted collapse from brutal 1949 blizzards to grow into a five-rig operation by 1951. That's the year True, along with Douglas S. Brown, bought out the other owners of Reserve Drilling and formed a partnership known as True and Brown Drilling Contractors, which set in motion a series of changes, culminating with the formations of True Drilling Company and True Oil Company.

Dave and I hit it off from the get-go.

In addition to Dave and Jean True, Reva and I have been mightily blessed with some extraordinary friendships resulting from our involvement with IPAA…Jack and Rita Allen, A.V. and Pat Jones Jr. and Jon Rex and Ann Jones to just mention a few. One invaluable treasure I discovered in my earliest involvement with IPAA was my buddy A.V. Jones Jr. of Albany, Texas, as we forged what was to become a lifelong friendship. Over the years we would become business associates and, in some cases, partner up on projects. We are still in regular contact to this day.

One of the reasons A.V. and his younger brother, Jon Rex, and I became such tight buddies was the uncanny mirror images of our backgrounds. Somebody did an article on A.V. once and mentioned our friendship, delineating fourteen similarities, including:

- Both from longtime oil families—he's third generation in Texas; I'm second generation in Michigan.
- Both independent oil and gas producers from relatively small towns whose name begins with A—Albany, Texas; Allegan, Michigan.
- Both in the business with brothers—Jon Rex; and Gene and Jack.
- Both early employers of seismic in our respective states.
- Both with a deep and unambiguous faith in the Almighty, who guides our every personal and business decision. (In fact, our initial acquaintance came about through the prayer breakfasts held in conjunction with IPAA meetings.)
- Both devoted to our industry and committed to perpetuating, protecting and advocating for the independent oil and gas exploration and production industry.

With Gene and A. V. Jones Jr. at a 1984 Michigan public auction of lease rights to State-owned mineral rights in Lansing, Michigan.

Of all the honors and accolades and gifts I've received in my career, I want this to be crystal clear: knowing and working with A.V. Jones Jr. has been precious beyond simple words to me, a friendship of inestimable value, facilitated by our joint association with IPAA. And integral to that have been the times we've shared with A.V. and his wife Pat in Michigan, and in Texas, and in traveling around the globe together. Even to this day, the Millers of Michigan and the Jones family of Texas remain the best of friends. The next generation, my son Mike and A.V.'s son K.C., have picked up the family friendship tradition by co-planning the Annual Father/Son Quail Hunting trip in Georgia.

Gene, Jack and I, along with our wives, began attending IPAA events which swung wide a number of other doors, exposing us to deals all across the country, and I will forever thank Vance Orr Sr. for opening that initial gate and shoving us through it, as that moment thrust us onto a new and higher platform in our history as a company and as individuals.

My interest in and involvement with IPAA and its goals continued to flourish. With the friendship and tutelage of people like Harold McClure Jr., Dave True, A. V. Jones Jr., Vance Orr Sr., Bill Brown, and Allan Morrow, my circle of friends on the national level broadened dramatically. I liked what they had to say and apparently they reciprocated the feeling.

In October 1967, during my second year as president of MOGA, I watched as Harold M. McClure Jr. became the 17th president of IPAA, elected at age 46. Harold was the first from Michigan chosen to that prestigious office, serving in 1968 and 1969. I was proud to be among the Michigan contingent at that Houston, Texas, meeting along with

Mike Cameron, Gerald Eddy, I. W. "Bucky" Hartman, brother Gene, Stuart "Shorty" Merrill, Vance Orr Sr., Chuck Smith, Charles Stewart, Fred Turner and Jay Woods to hear Harold accept the IPAA presidency with words that echoed my own sentiment.

"The IPAA has long been a cornerstone of this industry. It has been a strong advocate of the proper use of every talent available to maintain a strong industry, a strong producing segment, so our nation can enjoy an adequate supply of petroleum at a reasonable cost to the people of the United States.

We must continue to recognize the changing technology, which is changing our industry. I, for one, do not believe in the status quo. Our membership must change to meet the changes. We'll see some fertile opportunities for independents over the next decade, a reawakening of attitude. This reawakening will be among those in policy-making positions in government and in the public in recognition of the validity and policies which IPAA has long nurtured...the necessity of maintaining a strong domestic oil and gas industry."

Over three decades, I served in a variety of IPAA roles: as director, vice president, member of the executive committee, chairman of the membership advisory committee, chairman of the supply-and-demand committee, and as a member of the import policy committee.

I also became an officer in a sister organization of IPAA—the National Stripper Well Association (NSWA)—which represents producers and operators of marginally economic crude oil and natural gas wells in the United States called stripper wells, which comprise nearly eighty percent of all United States domestic wells and produce about twenty percent of U.S. oil and natural gas. I was elected NSWA president for 1971-1972. Membership on the National Petroleum Council and American Petroleum Institute rounded out my oil industry affiliations. Closer to home, I served on the Michigan Oil and Gas Advisory Board, a technical support group to the Michigan Geological Survey Chief and Supervisor of Wells.

Still, I don't want anyone thinking I was such a single-minded, gung-ho fanatic for work that I let it eclipse the rest of my life. I did a stint as chairman of the Grand Rapids Baptist College and Seminary (now Cornerstone University) Executive Board. My mother, Verna, served the same school for many years as a dorm mother for Miller Hall (named after her), so that institution became especially close to our hearts. As the Lord's blessings made more and more resources available, Gene and I were also fortunate to be able to assist with funding the Miller Library for our beloved Cornerstone.

During these hectic years I also served as president of the Allegan Board of Education; as trustee on the Board of the Directors of the Michigan National Bank of Grand Rapids; and as trustee on the Board of Directors of Allegan General Hospital.

All this time, Reva and I were raising a son and three daughters. We had the summer place on Gull Lake and engaged through the years in a vast variety of activities: snowmobiling and boating, bicycling and golf, tennis and basketball. All of us enjoyed riding our Tennessee Walking horses as well. Reva and I even engaged in a little motorcycling, but quit before sustaining some near-death experience in the form of mangled steel and twisted tires.

I served as chairman of the board of deacons and as Sunday school teacher at First Baptist in Allegan, which our families all attended. Reva taught Sunday school; Gene and Betty were heads of the finance committee; Jack served as a greeter. So church became our own form of Miller-time, a Baptist family affair.

In 1973 I became the second Michigan oilman elected president of IPAA—right at the time Michigan was in the throes of economic frustration. Our Niagaran Pinnacle Reef production was doing just fine, the result in large measure of our utilization of seismic data to locate and drill into those magnificent rock-encased pinnacle reefs with a gratifying proportion of them bearing oil and gas. We had production in Mason County and had done a bunch of seismic work aimed at developing our acreage in Manistee County, and we had interests running pretty much across the arc comprising the Northern Michigan Niagaran Reef Trend.

But there was a problem—a staggering problem: we couldn't sell the oil from many of those wells because they were so isolated from pipelines. In order to produce the oil you must get rid of the natural gas—by pipeline. You can truck oil, but there ain't no truckin' natural gas.

In earlier times, we could flare-off the natural gas when quantities were small. But the Niagaran reefs were spilling over with it, rendering flaring both out of the question generally, and outside the boundaries of the law itself as the state imposed a no-flare order for northern Michigan. Compounding that frustration was the problem of low wellhead prices (the price we could get for our production), a malady afflicting independents not just in Michigan, but all over the country.

The week before the Houston, Texas, IPAA meeting, when I would assume the office of president on October 20, 1973, I was interviewed for the Petroleum Independent magazine (now defunct, but then the official publication of the Independent Petroleum Association of America) by Lloyd Unsell, who served IPAA from 1948 until he retired in 1987 as its president and chief executive. Lloyd had worked as a reporter for the Seminole (Oklahoma) Producer and Tulsa World until 1948, when he joined the oil industry association as a staff writer in Tulsa. In 1964, he moved to Washington and served initially as executive vice-president, until he became its president and chief executive in 1976. So he was one tough interviewer.

Lloyd asked, "Here in Washington a lot of people seem to think we haven't got much more oil left for production domestically in the United States. What's your feeling about that?"

"I think that's an erroneous view," I replied, "and I don't know that anybody agrees with the U.S. Geological Survey as to the amount of production that can be found (that fault-riddled survey had predicted America had only five years of oil left for discovery—and had propounded the same ominous number every year since 1918). I've heard some argument that they're a little optimistic. But let's say they are partially correct. If they are, there's a tremendous amount of resource to be developed right here, and that's a story told time and time and time again. If economic incentives are correct, production will be found." [14]

Thirty-seven years later, I can't think of a way I'd change that statement. It is a simple formula: the more you drill the more you are likely to find, and anything that discourages drilling decreases the amount of oil and gas you will discover.

---

[14] Appendix F - 1973 Oil Pricing and Political Controls

At the end of the interview, Lloyd asked, "Do you have any idea what you'll do as IPAA president?"

"I don't see any big problems or have some great philosophy of operation or anything," I answered. "I am personally convinced that the next few years will be the most interesting period the oil and gas industry will have experienced in a long time, especially with a universal recognition of our irrefutable energy crisis. The possible movement of price, the possible restriction of Canadian oil flow to the United States, dealing with the deregulation of natural gas—all of these have coalesced since the beginning of this calendar year.

"We are also going to have to deal with trying to get a situation where oil can be priced at a competitive market level instead of some old oil/new oil type situation.

"I think all these obstacles have to be cleared out of the way, and oil and gas prices have to come right along to a level where they are competitive with other energy forms and where people can get at finding the resources. I would hope also to educate folks as to the danger of caving in to rabid environmentalists at the cost of our well being now and in the future.

"It is a nationwide effort, not a matter of let's drill up the sparsely populated southern states while we sit under a tree and drink in nature instead of developing in an orderly manner the oil and gas under the more north-woodsy, nature-laden states where the majority of opposition to drilling seems to originate."

At the end of the interview, Lloyd asked how our business was run. I said we felt our involvement in the industry was substantial, with tight focus on the educational aspects, and with caution about not spreading ourselves too thin. I also told him about the Bible verse we patterned our business after: ***"And whatsoever ye do in word or deed, do all in the name of the Lord Jesus, giving thanks to God the Father by Him."*** ***(Colossians 3:17)*** True then. True now.

I felt energized at the conclusion of our dialogue, felt I had weathered without misstep Lloyd's battery of questions. But there was no way I could have prophesied what the next week would bring.

INDEPENDENT PETROLEUM ASSOCIATION OF AMERICA

Saturday evening, October 20, 1973, at age 42, I became the 20th president of the Independent Petroleum Association of America (IPAA) at a banquet held at the old Shamrock Hilton Hotel in Houston, Texas. It was a date the world would never forget, not because of my induction, but because of two concurrent events of international magnitude.

There was, first, a traumatic government upheaval in the Watergate crisis, as President Nixon discharged Special Prosecutor Archibald Cox and accepted the resignations of Attorney General Elliot L. Richardson and Deputy Attorney General William D. Ruckelshaus. Simultaneously, the president abolished the office of the special prosecutor and turned over to the Justice Department all responsibility for further investigation and for prosecution of suspects and defendants in Watergate and related cases.

Second, in the Middle East, the members of OAPEC (Organization of Arab Petroleum Exporting Countries), consisting of the Arab members of OPEC (Organization of Petroleum Exporting Countries), along with Egypt and Syria, announced an oil embargo "in response to the U.S. decision to re-supply the Israeli military" during the Yom Kippur War. OAPEC declared it would limit or stop oil shipments to the United States and other countries supporting Israel in the conflict. The embargo would last until March 1974.

I remember hearing the story about my friend Tom Mask returning to his hotel room later that evening and turning on the television set just in time to hear a reporter signing off saying, "Never in my twenty years at this desk have I had two such monumental events to report in a single newscast." This was long before 24/7 television news, so Tom couldn't just wait a half an hour for the next broadcast to find out what had prompted the newsman's ominous comment. His only recourse was to race from his room and spend the next hour buttonholing folks, seeking information in a futile attempt to fill in the gaping blanks.

Next morning the IPAA Imports Committee Chairman opened its meeting, saying, "For the first time in our thirty-nine year history, we have nothing to report."

Immediately everything energy-related kicked into high gear. All industrialized economies relied on crude oil, and OPEC was their primary supplier. Because of the dramatic inflation experienced during this period, some contended that these price increases were to blame for suppressing economic activity. Others argued that targeted countries ought to respond with a variety of new initiatives to contain further dependency. The 1973 oil price shock, in concert with the 1973-74 stock market crash, stands as the first event since the Great Depression of 1929 to have a truly sustained economic effect. They were a thunderous pair of earthquakes—with all sorts of horrific after-shocks.

I knew when I took the job of IPAA president I'd have to testify before Congress a couple of times over my two-year term—and that would provide a good platform for educative dialogue with legislators. But as oil prices shot up after being depressed more than twenty years, I found myself in the hot seat testifying dozens of times—far more than anyone in the oil business ever had before.

Lloyd Unsell noted of those years: "The liberal agenda turned into a crusade to break up the big oil companies; to start a federal oil and gas company; and to rigidly regulate oil and natural gas prices, supply and distribution. John Miller articulated a consistent, no-nonsense argument that the less government, the better.

"Rumors were flying of tankers laden with oil basking in the Chesapeake Bay waiting for prices to go up still higher. Forcibly disputing this nonsense far more effectively than anyone else, John Miller emerged as an acknowledged industrial statesman across the country."

I traveled the country talking to groups of independents, press reporters, the general public and politicos. Suddenly it became my job to teach the rudimentary economics of the oil and gas business to folks who wanted everything condensed into thirty-second sound bytes.

It amazes me to this day that people know more about the life of an athlete or film celebrity than they do about where their paycheck comes from and about the costs of doing business incurred by the people who serve them with supplies and commodities. Illiteracy, I'm convinced, comes in a multiplicity of guises.

"The big problem," I would tell those who railed against the oil business in derisive clichés as they queued up waiting to pay ever higher, ever spiraling pump prices, "is that our industry did such a great job for so long satisfying the nation's growing petroleum appetite that they forgot to ask how much it cost...and we forgot to tell them."

I hammered home again and again the dangers of the U.S. importing thirty-seven percent of its crude oil consumption (by 2009, that number had soared to more than sixty-eight percent) and emphasized that unless tax policy changed, our reliance on imports would never retreat to an acceptable level.

In the face of the Windfall Profits Tax, a confiscatory levy designed to punish domestic oil producers while world prices dictated by OPEC went unchecked, I laid out a plan, maintaining that an energy tax policy should be designed to:

- Extend the economic life of existing energy-producing properties;
- Encourage development of discovered but undeveloped high-cost reserves;
- Stimulate investment in wildcat drilling to expand producible reserves;
- Attract the investment of risk capital from outside the petroleum industry;

- Recognize the ever-rising costs of replacing energy supplies currently consumed and the need to overcome the inertia of years of declining exploration and development.

Guess how the federal government reacted. It perpetuated the Windfall Profits Tax and replaced the complicated new-oil/old-oil/stripper-oil pricing structure with an even more Byzantine upper-tier/lower-tier/world-price system, thrusting the price we could get for our production into such a quagmire of confusion that sometimes it would vacillate depending on whether the trucks came to pick up the oil in the morning or the afternoon. Petroleum accountants did their best to keep us out of trouble, but later there would be accusations of tax-dodging (alongside the price-gouging cry of the uninformed) over simple misunderstandings of when the oil was sold, discovered or produced.

I maintained that in order for America to secure our domestic energy supply, we should formulate a policy taking into account basic characteristics of oil and gas exploration and production including:

- Exploration for the development of crude oil and natural gas resources is both capital-intensive and high risk;
- Long lead times before investment generates any significant returns can compound both the risk and the capital requirements;
- Unlike most industrial enterprises, the successful ventures (producing wells) must not only be self-sustaining, but also pay for unsuccessful ventures (dry holes).

Congress effected moderate changes in the tax acts, but the tone of most legislation was punitive to the oil and gas industry, reflecting a politically expedient attempt to appease the outrage of a confused and misinformed public.

The fall of 1973 was a turbulent time for all Americans, but especially those occupying the political landscape of Washington, D.C. In late 1973, President Nixon named Gerald Ford to replace scandal-plagued Vice-President Spiro Agnew, declaring how he'd selected Ford for his reputation as a congressman of unblemished integrity and unwavering trustworthiness. Off the record some suggested he was chosen more because his blandness made him palatable to both the left and right. But I'm convinced that key to the appointment was the fact that he and Nixon had been friends since the mid-1950s.

Into this arena I entered the Washington, D.C. scene as president of the Independent Petroleum Association of America. I knew Vice-President Ford from having met with him years earlier when he served in the U.S. House of Representatives as a Michigan congressman, wielding the title Minority House Whip. In July, 1974, as IPAA president, I arranged for a contingent of Michigan oil folk to have lunch with Vice-President Ford. Everybody showed up, save Ford. I felt disappointed and confused since he had always been a stand-up guy who followed through when he committed to do something or be somewhere. As it happened, our scheduled luncheon with him was the very day he received word he was to become the new president of the United States, so he had lofty, urgent matters pressing upon him. Later he called and apologized.

Ford had served as Nixon's vice-president for just eight months, until the Watergate cover-up compelled Nixon's resignation, whereupon Ford was sworn in as president on August 9, 1974.

Ford subsequently made some very tough decisions, especially his pardoning of the disgraced and fallen President Nixon, and his welcoming back of draft dodgers who had fled military service in Vietnam. In the end he brought, I'm convinced, healing to a wounded and hurting nation and closure to one of our saddest chapters.

In October of 1975 at the World Energy Conference held at Detroit's Cobo Hall, Ford declared war on foreign crude oil imports with what he called Project Energy Independence. Though he sought to implement some policies that would aid our industry (and thus promote the nation's energy security), he really accomplished little on that front.[15]

1975 – At the White House, I discuss our domestic oil and gas industry with President Gerald R. Ford.

President Ford and I got along well in those unsettling years he served in office. He took genuine interest in the problems of the domestic oil and gas exploration and production industry and did his best against a resistant Congress to ensure our nation's future energy security. Rumors abounded that if Ford had been elected president in 1976, I would be on his short list of prospective candidates for energy secretary. It was a flattering thought, but of course, could never materialize.

---

[15] Appendix G – President Ford's Proposed Legislation

As president, Ford signed the Helsinki Accord, marking a lengthy step toward detente in the Cold War. With the conquest of South Vietnam by North Vietnam nine months into his presidency, U.S. involvement in Vietnam essentially ended. Domestically, Ford presided over what constituted at the time the worst economy since the Great Depression, with swelling inflation and a nasty recession during his tenure. In 1976, he narrowly defeated Ronald Reagan for the Republican nomination, but ultimately lost the presidential election to Democrat Jimmy Carter.

Over the next several years I met with Presidents Ford, Reagan, Carter, and Bush along with other U.S. senators and congressmen on the issue of national energy policy.

President Gerald R. Ford died December 26, 2006, in California, at 93. His passing rekindled my warm memories of him, a man of highest character in our country's highest office, always so kind and approachable. Much of the historic commentary regarding Mr. Ford's presidency references the fact that he was the only person to serve as vice-president and president without being elected to either office.

Early in my career in Washington, I was scheduled to meet one morning with a congressional contingent about the U.S. oil industry at large. I presumed I would be the only one testifying, but it turned out Amoco Oil Company Chairman, John Swearingen, was also there—and thought likewise, that he would be flying solo with his remarks before the committee.

But we discovered quickly that committee members were aiming to conduct their fact-finding in one sitting, so there were five major oil companies in the world at that time all set to testify…and then there was me. There were several companies combined into each session, all represented by their respective CEO's and attendant staffs.

U. S. Congressional committee, one of the many times I testified during my 1973-1974 tenure as IPAA President. Note the near-empty room. Both the press and the public focused more on scandal-mongering headlines than in the truths elicited in these hearings.

Conversely, I was there by my lonesome, as usual, because I preferred to make my own points without dragging a lot of the IPAA administration around with me, and Lloyd Unsell and legal counsel Dan Jones concurred on the strategy as we sought to underline the David-versus-Goliath disparity between us independents and the high-profile majors. Swearingen, chairman of the American Petroleum Institute (representing major oil companies), became upset he'd not learned beforehand the format for giving testimony. He was especially chagrined over the protocol of the proceedings and voiced his disdain in such a way that people thought he was angry with me and with the notion that a diminutive organization like IPAA should be included in such high-level hearings. I didn't read his displeasure as a personal affront to me and my organization, so I let it go and refused to get as rattled as everybody else.

Sometime later when I was attending a meeting in Texas, Swearingen walked up to me.

"Where are you heading?" he asked.

"Back to Michigan," I told him.

"Why don't you come with me on our corporate jet, and I'll drop you in Chicago so your plane can pick you up there," he suggested.

I readily accepted. By this time I was traveling across the country so often that we had acquired our own airplane and hired full-time pilot Walt Buchko to shuttle me about on business trips. So Swearingen's gracious offer saved us a lot of time and money, to say nothing about airport aggravations. On the flight to Chicago, Swearingen and I got to know each other far better, visiting about a number of subjects, and he proved himself to be an exceptional friend as the years unfolded.

I learned a strong lesson from that experience: don't let one niggling incident determine and cement your position about any individual. Situations change and you need to keep doors open and be as friendly as you can with everyone. That precept has stood us in good stead with companies and individuals beyond count.

Let me add a footnote to the "flying" theme. Some years prior to the Swearingen incident, Gene had acquired his private pilot license while Mike was in the process of earning his, under instructor Frank Geib. Naturally, I caught the bug and assumed it would be best for me to get licensed too. But Gene and Mike were quick to dissuade me, explaining that while I had soloed, I never ever practiced on my own, and that with my tendency to be in a perpetual rush to get somewhere I wouldn't take the imperative precautions that would ensure my flying safety. I knew they were right. So in the end it was unanimous: I would stick with what I did best—being passenger, not pilot.

RETURN TO ALLEGAN WITH PUBLIC LIFE DONE... I THINK

The evening of October 27, 1975, I turned over the reins of the IPAA presidency to my good friend A. V. Jones Jr. at our annual membership meeting in Dallas. I began my farewell address with a nod to the countless hotel nights I had spent on the road circumnavigating the United States as spokesman for independent oil and gas producers. "No more free soap from now on," I told Reva. I stuck those tumultuous two years in the rearview mirror, knowing that I would miss the action, that there was still so much to do, and that an immediate past president was, by definition, hamstrung and confined to pasture. At the same time I knew categorically that A.V. Jones Jr. was up to grabbing the baton from me and running hard the next critical leg of our race. He had to be.

Acrimony toward our industry spewed out on multiple fronts—from public, press and politicians—reaching epic proportions as crude oil prices and gasoline pump prices

OCTOBER 27, 1975 A. V. Jones Jr., incoming IPAA President, looks on as Harold M. McClure Jr. bids me farewell as IPAA President.

continued to escalate. The whole scene was starting to assume the frenetic passion of a lynch mob.

As my term wound to its close, I hoped I had served my fellow petroleum independents well and soon got the surprise of my life when it came time for the annual presentation of Lone Star Steel's Chief Roughneck Award.[16] Lone Star Steel had begun presenting this honor in 1955 for lifetime achievement, recognizing those distinguished individuals who have left their indelible mark on the petroleum industry. Only the truly greats of our business had received this award—the Dave Trues, the H. L. Hunts, the L. B. Meaders. It was a short, prestigious list.

I fought off shock when I heard these words: "Scan the horizon or rub elbows, check the news media, listen in on a quick conversation, visit the halls of Congress, or even the president's office. Do all those things and more, and nowhere will you find anyone in the petroleum industry more highly praised for his stand on the nation's energy problem than the 1975 Chief Roughneck, John Miller.

"Articulate without being flamboyant, sincere in his presentation of hard facts and figures, utterly devoid of any self-serving motive except to help the industry into which he was born, Miller has spent the past two years establishing a record of political action that is without equal in the annals of the oil patch.

"Knowledge of oildom and what makes it flow is no happenstance for John whose father, Clyde, was a boiler tender in the oil fields of West Virginia and progressed into contract drilling. Upon his death, John and his brother Clyde Junior ("Gene") organized the Miller Brothers partnership with two rigs from their father's estate. Another brother, Jack, serves as general manager in the company, which has production operations in the Niagaran Reef areas of Michigan's 'little north slope.'

"John's hometown, Allegan, Michigan, hasn't seen much of him during his two-year stint as IPAA's 20th president.

"Roughneck? You bet! We are proud of our own John Miller."

I know I looked flummoxed as I received the award for Rough and Rugged Service in the Field. I must have done an adequate job for the industry because the gracious words and acknowledgements kept coming as I stepped away from two years of service as president of IPAA.[17]

---

[16] Appendix H - Citations and Awards
[17] Appendix I – Independent Petroleum Association of America (IPAA)

BACK IN THE IPAA HARNESS...AGAIN

Still, I must not have done a superlative job protecting the industry, try as I did, as evidenced by what happened next. I returned to Allegan and immersed myself in our oil and gas exploration and production interests. But I sorely itched for the front-line action, missed defending our industry from the bully pulpit of the IPAA presidency.

James Earl "Jimmy" Carter Jr. served as 39th President of the United States from 1977 to 1981. He was a peanut farmer from Georgia, and so it was thought he would be in sympathy with those of us in the business world. So much for expectations, dashed as a result of rampant distrust in our domestic petroleum industry as articulated by liberal Democrats in Congress, by the press and by the general public.

As president, Carter created a new cabinet-level department: the Department of Energy. He established a putative national energy policy that included conservation, price controls, and new technology. In 1980 the United States enacted the Crude Oil Windfall Profit Tax Act (P.L. 96-223) as part of a compromise between the Carter administration and Congress over the decontrol of crude oil prices. The act was intended to recoup the revenue earned by oil producers as a result of the sharp increase in prices catalyzed by the OPEC oil embargo. According to the Congressional Research Service (CRA), the Act's title was a misnomer. "Despite its name," the CRA noted, "the crude oil windfall profit tax was not a tax on profits. It was really an excise tax imposed on the difference between the market price of oil—technically referred to as the *removal price*—and a statutory 1979 base price that was adjusted quarterly for inflation and state severance taxes."

By 1980, Carter's disapproval ratings were significantly higher than his approval metrics, prompting Ted Kennedy to challenge him for the Democratic nomination that year. Carter defeated Kennedy, but ultimately lost the general election to Republican Ronald Reagan.

About the same time IPAA made an unexpected and unprecedented move at their October meeting in New Orleans by amending their constitution to create a new position for the IPAA elected leader—chairman of the board of directors. They also chose a new long-term president to serve for an indefinite period of time, acting as chief operating officer. Under this structure, IPAA membership selected me to serve as its president. Lloyd Unsell was re-elected IPAA executive vice-president so I had my trusted friend riding shot-gun, as well as having at my disposal the ready skills of other staff, including the Washington, D.C., trio of Joe Farmer, 1973-1975 membership chairman and 1980 vice-president administration; Dan Jones Sr., our legal guru; and young Barry Russell, just coming on board to assist with membership. So I knew I had a formidable staff...both at IPAA in Washington D.C., and at Miller Brothers in Allegan, Michigan.

This newly established position required I establish residency in D.C. in order to act as IPAA's representative, so Reva and I moved into the infamous Watergate Condominiums. Senator Russell Long lived in the same complex as did Senator Robert

Dole and his wife, Elizabeth, who was on the White House staff. I walked daily to the IPAA offices, while Reva moved easily around Washington in her car.

For the next year I was back in my element. Once again I was on the road defending our industry against those who would decimate it through their aggressive ignorance. Because IPAA had a comprehensive plan oriented toward increased domestic energy production, I was able to communicate effective strategy and make some inroads in Congress.[18] Requisite amendments in the Fuel Tax Act became the objective of IPAA. We effected some changes, though not in the form we initially intended. Nonetheless, it was an auspicious start and other improvements would follow.

We pushed forward. We persuaded Reagan to rectify some glaring inequities in the President's Tax Act, in large measure because of the foundation, direction and urgency of IPAA's energy tax policy.

In retrospect, I feel unspeakably blessed by the wide assortment of contacts and opportunities Reva and I were privileged to engage over the panorama of those IPAA years. It was a time that zipped past, super-charged with excitement and challenge, our calendars jammed, sort of like sprinting a marathon.

Once Ashland Oil invited us to be their guests for the most prestigious of all horse-racing venues—the Kentucky Derby. No sooner had we landed at the airport than company officials grabbed our bags and whisked us off by limo for a sumptuous breakfast, followed by a scenic paddleboat ride down the river. Arriving later at our hotel room, we discovered the ultimate in maid service: our luggage unpacked, all our clothes smartly put away.

---

[18] Appendix J - Congressional Testimony Record

The days leading up to the Derby swirled with entertainment options, including visits to luxurious horse farms, most notably Calumet, home of triple-crown winner Secretariat. Reva and I, along with equestrian friends Hank and Karen True, marveled over how immaculate the barns were, all absolutely radiant, gleaming with polish.

Other Ashland guests came from diverse walks of life, ranging from key politicians to compatriots in the oil and gas industry to horse aficionados to the reigning Miss America, who had represented Kentucky in that year's pageant. (I stifled the impulse to ask for clarification of an ancient adage: whether Kentucky was the home of "fast horses and beautiful women," or of "beautiful horses and fast women?")

Of course, perfect seats at the Derby served as predictable climax to our series of highlights that Kentucky weekend and, as a final gift, Ashland Oil later sent us a pictorial catalog of all the events, rendering permanent our incredible memories.

Another time Mo Benson, on behalf of Atlantic Richfield (ARCO), invited Reva and me to tour their expansive Alaskan facilities. To our chagrin the day we were scheduled to fly commercial out of Kalamazoo a mammoth snowstorm buried the area, blocking our departure. I called Mo, advised him that getting out right then was impossible, that we'd have to forego the trip. Imagine my amazement when he declared, "If the Millers aren't able to attend, nobody's going to attend." At that point it became clear to me: sole purpose of the trip was to introduce us to ARCO's operation.

Swiftly, Mo made his next move. He arranged for a private jet to pick us up in Kalamazoo and fly us to the West Coast where the president of ARCO met us and then accompanied us to Alaska. Once there we were provided with weather appropriate attire—coats, boots, hats, gloves, etc. We had an instructive time examining their extensive layout, but the weather was so bone-chilling that vehicles were kept running 24/7 to prevent them from freezing up. (Little wonder Reva and I today have such abiding affection for Florida's sunshine…)

On a separate occasion ARCO's corporate generosity even provided us with a helicopter ride to one of their off-shore rigs, followed by a visit to the Los Angeles Olympics. So some of the majors—but most notably Ashland and ARCO—treated us with extraordinary kindness.

There were, as well, social occasions with presidents, providing us with rare, behind-the-scenes glimpses. During Ronald Reagan's presidency, we received an invitation to the White House, and after the president had concluded his introductory remarks, Reva and I found ourselves standing beside First Lady Nancy Reagan. Suddenly a woman outside the circle of White House security moved toward Mrs. Reagan and urgently began presenting her concerns. Ever gracious, Nancy promised to convey her petition to the president.

A short time later, as Reagan himself was passing by, the same lady pressed forward, seized his arm, and began stating her case. Immediately—instinctively—Nancy pulled loose the lady's hand and tactfully said, "I told you I would pass along your concerns. Now get back behind security." Reva and I, right there beside Mrs. Reagan, had witnessed the entire scene, had heard the exact, terse dialogue. However, when next morning's news recounted the incident, it reported how Nancy was snooty and pushy and out of order, all of which confirmed how we must be vigilant in our discernment of the media, refusing to accept in full faith its often glorified gossip.

U.S. Secretary of the Interior James G. Watts discusses energy policy possibilities with Reva and me at an IPAA reception in 1981.

Another time while I was in California on IPAA business, I received an invitation from friends to join them for dinner at the Reagan Ranch. When the call came that evening to be seated, I had remained standing, locked in deep dialogue with an oil and gas fellow from Kansas. All at once there was Ronald Reagan beside us, gesturing toward a small table, saying, "Looks like all the places are taken in the dining room. Why don't we eat right here." So the three of us sat down. Moments later singer Pat Boone strolled over and made it a fourth.

There was also a dicey moment in my association with Reagan when, enroute home from a hunting trip and carrying my rifle in its case, I checked into a hotel where I was scheduled to have breakfast the next morning with the president. Need I note how thoroughly the Secret Service scrutinized me there in the lobby? Next day, as I headed up to Reagan's floor, the elevator lurched to a stop, and there stood a cordon of agents blocking the door, looking me up and down and inside out. It all served as stark reminder: how mindful those in highest political office have to be for their security—as Ronald Reagan would one day learn way too up-close and way too personal.

I always found Reagan to be kind and cordial and empathetic, and later that same day he demonstrated his warm sensibility when I attended a meeting where he was set to address a group of women. When it was his time to speak, he apologized to them for their inconvenience of having to stand and wait so patiently for his delayed appearance.

Ronald Reagan, ever the gentleman.

George Herbert Walker Bush also left a singular impression. Once Reva and I had the honor of standing in a receiving line with him and Barbara. And on another occasion, while visiting the DeVos family in Holland, Michigan, Reva and I took a speedboat ride with the Bushes, with the president, in his full-throttle, athletic intensity at the helm, powering across Lake Michigan.

All at once a frantic voice came crackling through the radio: "Slow down! Please slow down! We can't keep up with you!" It was the Secret Service…less than pleased…reduced to pleading.

Still, in the midst of all our IPAA ventures, Reva and I continued to pursue our athletic passions—golf and tennis and biking—and to cultivate our rich Michigan relationships. For several years we traveled with good friends Bob and Sue Brown to Vermont for bicycle tours through autumn's exquisite colors—a week that combined strenuous exercise with excellent food and quaint bed-and-breakfasts.

Preparation for our annual trip out East was always arduous, as Reva and I would put in hard hours pounding down Michigan roads, often with Bob and Sue.

Our first bicycle trip east was laughably insightful. Bob is a former tight-end for the University of Michigan, an athletic wide-body, about a decade my junior. On one of our rides, I found myself right behind the big fella', snuggled up tight to his rear tire. I could tell he was working hard, breathing heavy. After a bit, he shouted out for me to come around and take the lead. I didn't budge, content to stay back, enjoying where I was, utterly oblivious to what I later learned to be biking protocol. I heard about that faux pas in spades from son Mike and his boys, all bikers. I had stayed in Bob's slipstream the whole time, drafting behind the ex-Wolverine as he beat against the wind. Bob never let me forget.

Reva pushed herself to the absolute edge that day, becoming so exhausted at one point that when we stopped at a little country store, she dismounted her bike and literally dropped down on the steps. At the same time an older gentleman arrived and stood by hesitantly, wondering how he was going to get up to the store. Reva just lay there, never budged. Finally, she looked up at the man through all her fatigue and said, "You're just going to have to step over me. I'm too tired to move."

That wasn't even the end of our drama. For lunch we ate some chili, which unsettled our stomachs for the rest of the ride and no doubt contributed to the nasty fall I later took, as I toppled over on the side of the road just as a huge bus came rumbling past. Scary doesn't begin to describe it…

All those IPAA years I was busy–busy and having a ball. I didn't know I was stressed… but God did. In January 1982, at age 50, I was laid low by that massive heart attack. My family remembers too well what transpired that morning I collapsed at the office. They 911'd the ambulance that rushed me to Allegan General's E.R., where I arrived disoriented, vulnerable, fragile and in pain. What followed over the next ten hours was a tight monitoring of my vitals, which refused to calm down and stabilize. It was then the recommendation of long-time family physician, Dr. Jim Wheat, that I be transferred immediately to Blodgett Hospital in Grand Rapids with its state-of-the-art cardio equipment. But snow, wind and ice conspired to make the transport a huge challenge, forcing the ambulance to the side of the highway periodically for the scraping of its windshield. Following behind, Reva and Mike and Pam even wondered if I had passed. They—and the girls—all insisted later that I had always represented their pillar-of-strength, their go-to guy, the indestructible one who held the Miller clan together. Suddenly that perception changed, and for the first time they saw me exactly as I was: a mere mortal fighting for life.

As I came out of the crisis, my cardiologist at Blodgett summarized the heart attack's cause: stress. I objected to his assessment, told him to the contrary. "I have no stress," I insisted. "My wife manages our family very well. I love, absolutely love, my work. I utterly enjoy my life."

He followed up by asking me to encapsulate what all had gone on the few days prior to my episode. I told him: Reva and I had recently returned to Michigan from a trip to Alaska to observe oil finds, including a tour of Prudhoe Bay, with ARCO; then we'd made a quick trip to Washington, D.C., to address political issues...But those were things I savored doing. Nothing stressful.

The doctor then explained gently—almost diplomatically—how a person can have stress even from doing too much of what he best loved. I confessed to him I had to plead guilty to that charge.

In the course of my recovery, it became all too clear I would either have to slow down or just not be here anymore. I labeled it a compulsory return to private life. So it was back to Allegan, where changes beyond my control were soon to pop.

At a MOGA Picnic in the early 1980s – my "back-up team" who kept Miller Brothers running at home while I criss-crossed the United States as IPAA President: my son Mike, Gene's son Kelly, Jack and Gene.

DIFFERENT DIRECTIONS:
MILLER ENERGY, INC. AND MILLER OIL CORPORATION

In 1985, after thirty-one years of continuous operation in Allegan in a partnership, Gene and I determined to pursue further activities as two separate entities. Involvement of our sons in the business and their respective desires to approach various aspects of the industry with diverse styles and differing philosophies, led to our taking different but equal paths.

Gene and I concurred all along about divine vision: whatever map God laid out clearly was the only right course for us—individually and jointly. To that end, Mike and I formed Miller Energy, Inc. and opened offices in Kalamazoo, Michigan, several miles south of Allegan. Gene and Kelly moved their families north to Traverse City, Michigan, and formed Miller Oil Corporation (not to be confused with Miller BROTHERS Oil Corporation), now known as Eagle Investments. Concurrently, Jack headed to Grand Rapids from where he deftly managed the legal and legislative affairs for the remaining assets of both Miller Brothers Partnership and Miller Brothers Oil Corporation. Over the ensuing years, Miller Energy and Eagle Investments have continued to work together in many ventures while each company has pursued other discrete interests.

In 1998, Miller Energy sold both its Michigan production and its producing properties to Conoco, Inc. That sale allowed us to concentrate fully on exploring and developing our leasehold inventory. Miller Energy continued aggressively spreading out in the Michigan Basin and began expanding our efforts beyond, eventually partnering with five other independent oil companies to form Global Exploration Company (GLOBEX), an international oil and gas exploration and production firm.

Jack, meanwhile, made it a complete set of Miller brothers to become elected chief executive of MOGA, when he served as chairman of the board in 1988-1989.

Continuing the family tradition, son Mike served as MOGA chairman 2000-2001. Then in 2009, Mike's son Luke became the fourth generation of Millers to join MOGA, and two of Gene's grandsons, Adam and Chad, followed suit. Today that multiple-generation assault stands as the historic record for a single family's membership in the organization. What an ineffable blessing—for Gene and me especially.

INTERNATIONAL TRAVELS
RUSSIA AND CHINA 1980s

In 1981, both the Chinese and Russian governments contacted the United States People-to-People program requesting that a representation of the U.S. independent oil and gas producers visit for a technical learning experience. Advised of this opportunity, IPAA chairman Kye Trout Jr. and his staff organized a delegation of independent oil industry personnel for the purpose of making ourselves, our experiences, and our knowledge available to the geologists, engineers and general oil industry people of China and Russia as well as having the opportunity of touring their oilfield operations.

The delegation, including Reva and me, Karney and Gertrude Cochran, Bill and Laura Geitz, A.V. Jr. and Pat Jones, Joseph and Barbara Kelly, D. A. and Peggy Kimball, William and Connie LeMay, Denny and Mary Long, Kye and Mary Trout, Cary Maquire; Ray Potts, H.G. "Bud" Scoggins, Bob Vinson and others traveled for three weeks the spring of 1982, touring Russia and China.

We spent the larger amount of time in Russia where we were assigned a guide named Zoya, who was high up in the Russian Oil Ministry. At first she was a touch standoffish, answering questions only with a guarded attitude as though we were suspicious characters.

One day she and I were locked into a conversation that I was recording for my own edification. Suddenly, Zoya became upset about the tape recorder, so I just handed it to her and said, "Here, keep it. We're not spying on you; I was just taking notes for myself." After that, her icy attitude thawed considerably. She had been trying hard to convince us everything in Russia was just fine until we noticed at one point a lot of idle construction cranes, and she finally conceded her country was bankrupt.

In short time she became such a friend that Reva and I arranged for her and her husband to visit the United States. Before we left, we promised to bring them to visit New York and Washington, D.C. Then they would be guests of Reva and me in Florida. Reva gave her a coat as a gift upon our departure from Russia about the same time we informed her of the arrangements we'd finalized for her tour of the States. The gift and the news overwhelmed Zoya, reducing her to tears because a visit to the United States was not possible without our help.

Their visit with us in Florida was a predictable delight as we escorted Zoya and her husband to some of the state's most popular sites, including Disney World. During the Disney parade they both broke into tears, their emotions triggered by an awareness that every American could freely enjoy someplace as remarkable and magical as Disney World, a luxury afforded by only the most affluent in their country.

Zoya's first encounter with an American restaurant menu was also provocative. "Do they really have all the things to eat that are listed here?" she asked. She explained how in Russia there might be a lot of options listed on a menu, but the restaurant would really have only one or two dishes available.

The China leg of our journey was also eye-opening although shorter in duration. Unfortunately we did not observe as much of the country's oilfield operations as we had seen of Russia's. The Chinese people were extremely kind and put us up in a huge private home in a park-like setting and accommodated us with spacious rooms. We visited the Great Wall of China and were feted at a number of banquets, most featuring fish. We urged the Chinese to think hard about collaborating with Americans on oil and gas development, but they were not overtly receptive, though much later they began working more with foreigners.

SAUDI ARABIA, IRAQ AND YEMEN

In 1990, Saudi Arabian Oil Minister Ali Naimi (who still serves in that position) visited the United States, interested in meeting with some of us at IPAA. I sat beside him at a formal dinner in Washington, D.C., and while we and our wives enjoyed identical meals in separate rooms—out of deference to Arab custom—Ali Naimi and I chatted about production volumes of a new well in Arabia that he was excited about.

"Boy, I'd like to see that one," I told him.

"Then why not come look it over," he replied.

"All I need is a formal invitation," I said, not expecting much since our previous attempts to enter Iraq to see their oil operations had been rebuffed.

"Done," he replied and made good his promise a few days later.

Saudi invitation in hand, I re-approached the Iraqis and this time received prompt sanction to tour their operations also. Dallas, Texas, independent oilman Ray L. Hunt had business revved up at the time near Sana'a, Yemen, and he encouraged us to tour that area, as well.

So it was that on March 5, 1991, fifteen of us—including IPAA chairman Paul Hilliard, George Alcorn, Sid Jansma Jr., Jack Allen, A.V. Jones Jr., Bud Scoggins, Gary Nicholson, and myself—set off on our first insightful tour of Middle East oil operations right as that tinderbox in world affairs was about to explode again into violence. Throughout our travels the atmosphere remained taut and foreboding. Armed guards checked and rechecked our identification countless times. They warned us repeatedly never, under any circumstance, to walk away from our briefcases—that any unattended luggage constituted a bomb threat. Thereafter we kept our cases tight at hand and watched, ready to run, for any of our bags that looked the least bit abandoned.

The air crackled with tension. One day while A. V. and I were walking around a park in Baghdad, Iraq, A. V. hauled out his camera and snapped a photo. Immediately a police car swung into surveillance mode and followed us all the way back to our hotel. American and European oil and gas people in Iraq confided that bombs and gunfire were essentially a daily occurrence there, which explained all the broken windows.

As we prepared to leave our Baghdad hotel, a young man offered to carry my luggage and spent much of the way to the lobby describing the horrors of life there, detailing the violent deaths of his friends and family while petitioning me to find a way to take him to the United States. Sadly, there was nothing I could do to help. I felt overwhelmed by his desperation.

The Saudis were gracious during our entire stay, and while their customs differ radically from ours, they seemed transparently pleased with our interest in their operations.

In Sana'a, Yemen, we were struck by the number of modern pickup trucks running around in a country fraught with poverty. When we had occasion to meet with the U.S. Ambassador to Yemen, he explained that a great many Yemenis had lived in the United States, mostly around Dearborn, Michigan, working in, and ultimately retiring from, the automobile industry, whereupon they returned to their home country, basking in comparative wealth from their American Social Security benefits.

My Middle East sojourn reinforced for me the blessings of our country. American petroleum producers/explorers who complain because we have to jump high hurdles trying to conduct business in the U.S. have no idea what adversity is until they've operated in a foreign country where corrupt bureaucracies run unchecked, where human life is incalculably cheap, and where each day is a rigorous exercise in survival. It's tragic we fail to comprehend how fortunate we are to live and work in America.

GLOBAL EXPLORATION, INC.

AN INTERNATIONAL EXPLORATION COMPANY

On the plane ride returning from that Middle East trip, A.V. and I got to talking about forming an international oil and natural gas exploration company. A group insisted they'd all be a part if I'd be its *Daddy*. I said I would.

And so came to be the conception and birth of the company we christened Global Exploration, Inc. (GLOBEX), with Gene and myself and the Jones brothers—A.V. and Jon Rex—along with Chuck Jacobs of Albany, Texas, and William C. Myler from Michigan, there at its earliest formation. I became its president, and we established our first office in Dallas in 1992, eventually moving operations to Houston.

GLOBEX operated and drilled in several foreign and remote countries including Australia, Papua New Guinea, Dutch North Sea, and Equatorial Guinea.

In 2000, I traveled to Equatorial Guinea with son Mike and grandson Jordan (thirteen years old) for the dedication of the electric plant, providing electricity to an otherwise antiquated country. As the afternoon progressed, I was somewhat startled to learn that the president of Equatorial Guinea had been watching the three of us throughout the day and now desired to meet with us personally. We were pleasantly surprised to discover the reason for his request: he was intrigued that three generations of the same family were standing before him—virtually unheard-of in Equatorial Guinea. He wanted his picture taken with us.

In time the stress of logistics, travel, and security made overseas operations more and more unwieldy than we cared to manage, so we sold GLOBEX—in all its glory—to Marathon Petroleum in 2002.

NORDHOUSE DUNES AREA CASE:

SETTING LEGAL PRECEDENT

Nowhere in our company's history did brother Jack prove his mettle—his tenacity and strength—so forcibly as he did in the Miller Brothers Oil Corporation (MBOC) legal action against the state of Michigan called the Nordhouse Dunes Law Suit. It all involved acreage leased by MBOC in Mason County near Ludington, Michigan.

The Nordhouse Dunes Area consists of 4,500 acres bordering four miles of Lake Michigan shoreline. Although the surface is owned primarily by the United States and is managed by the U.S. Forest Service, sixty-eight percent of its mineral rights are owned by private parties, twenty-four percent by the state of Michigan, and eight percent by the United States.

In 1983, we were preparing to move ahead and drill a well on acreage we had leased, land on which we had also completed substantial and costly seismic work. We felt confident we had a very strong opportunity of finding oil and gas here since we had already drilled successful wells to the north, south and east of the prospective acreage.

So we were holding compelling cards and knew the potential was enormous. The state of Michigan, however, squirmed under heavy political pressure from extremist environmental groups to preclude our drilling there because of its proximity to the Nordhouse Dunes. *Proximity* I underscore. *Near* the Nordhouse Dunes Area—not *on* them. Environmental opponents to drilling the acreage propounded the preposterous theory that we intended to bore right inside the dunes area, when in truth our plan was to drill a hole to a target-depth of more than seven thousand feet under the dunes from a surface location several hundred feet away using directional drilling technology.

Anyone with common sense would know that MBOC would never consider drilling *on* the dunes—would never even want to drill there—as it would have been too difficult and too costly to maneuver all requisite machinery and equipment into location on such soft sand. So we had long before concluded that drilling on the sand was utterly out of the question and never on the table, and clearly noted in our application to the state of Michigan for a permit our intention to drill that well by a sole technique—directional. We would be off the dunes and drill straight down to a predetermined depth, then bore in on the diagonal until we came to the point where we would drill vertically again, this time into the geological target zone we wanted to test.

This could be done—in truth, had been done—numerous times in Michigan without incident. The technique was nothing new, and was light years away from rocket science. This just pertained to plain common sense and should have been a routine matter. Drilling the hole would have been no different than boring hundreds of others in Michigan since the advent of directional-drilling technology a decade earlier. In fact, an earlier director of the Michigan Department of Natural Resources, Gene Gazlay (October

1972 – June 1974), had hailed directional drilling itself as a key answer to the problem of orderly development of Michigan's abundant petroleum resources in environmentally sensitive areas.

All of this logic counted for nothing in 1983 when we began negotiations with the state of Michigan. Shrill environmental extremists raised such hue and cry in opposition to the proposed hole that we commenced on what would turn into a four-year campaign of heavy paper-pushing to receive a drilling permit for the Nordhouse Dunes Area prospect.

In 1986, MBOC filed a proposed hydrocarbon development plan at the request of state officials, identifying five potential Niagaran Reef targets in the Nordhouse Dunes Area in Grant Township of Mason County. An inter-agency review team was formed, comprised of officials from the Michigan Department of Natural Resources and the U.S. Forest Service (which has jurisdiction over much of the surface within the Nordhouse Dunes Area), and the state authorized and requested an independent environmental impact study. The U.S. Forest Service approved drilling all five sites we had proposed in our development plan. The Michigan Department of Natural Resources held public hearings in Ludington, Lansing and Grand Rapids in January of 1987 to solicit comments on the state's Environmental Impact Statement concerning our proposed hydrocarbon-drilling plan. The Michigan Environmental Science Review Board recommended no drilling in certain portions of the Nordhouse Dunes Area but did not suggest a total ban on drilling. Still, the state remained adamant and refused to let us drill on the private acreage for which we had a legitimate working plan that exceeded requirements for drilling directional holes in an environmentally sensitive area. Running the show for us, Jack threatened the state with a lawsuit because we, as well as the private mineral owners in the acreage, were having our assets denied and stripped away.

Suddenly, with virtually zero warning, the state pulled the plug, breaking off all negotiations. The current Michigan Department of Natural Resource Director and Supervisor of Wells, Gordon Guyer, issued a determination on April 23, 1987, that drilling would not be "environmentally compatible with the unique natural features" of the area. This effectively vetoed our plan and prevented surface development of any kind in the 4,500-acre Nordhouse Dunes Area.

We had no choice: immediately we filed suit on behalf of Miller Brothers Oil Corporation and the private mineral owners within the Nordhouse Dunes Area, seeking $93 million as compensation for the mineral rights being denied for what we contended was reasonable and orderly development.

It was a gargantuan undertaking. Jack rode point the whole turbulent time, start to finish, warrior all the way, for which Gene and I were most grateful, as ancillary projects occupied most of our days. All the while Jack kept digging in his spurs. Every time you ran into him, all he talked about was the newest twist on the Nordhouse Dunes and the latest track of his pursuit. In the end all of Jack's persistence would pay off in spades.

On August 13, 1989, Court of Claims Judge Peter D. Houk granted us and our leased mineral owners motions for summary disposition and ordered the state of Michigan, as defendants, either to make restitution or rescind the April 23, 1987, order and allow drilling of the five sites approved earlier by the U.S. Forest Service.

The legal battle raged—a fierce, seven-week trial in September 1991. We retained John Jones of the Mika, Meyers, Beckett and Jones law firm in Grand Rapids as counsel. John was a superlative lawyer and an unsurpassed friend. (Now deceased, he left us in 2009 after a bout with cancer for a far better place, which St. Paul describes as the "*life that is truly life*.")

Jones managed to beat the state from every angle, making their attorneys look like first-year law students as the drama unfolded in front of a three-judge Appellate Court—with no attendant jury. It was critical we assemble our facts in such a way that the judges could comprehend the issues clearly and not become entrapped in intricacies the state kept trying to introduce regarding environmental sensitivity and emotional matters, all of which had nothing to do with the irrefutable facts of the science.

One day John Jones collared me. "You know, John, I think you and Judge Houk get along well. I want you to provide some input for the record."

"Leave me out of it," I said.

But John insisted.

At one point during my testimony, the judge asked, "Well, did Miller Brothers keep all the interest you ever had in this?"

I said, "No, we didn't."

"Why wouldn't you if you knew that it was going to be so valuable?" he asked.

"Knowing it had the potential to be valuable is a whole lot different than having the cash coming in by the month," I answered. "Ours is a risky business, a fact we've been acutely aware of all our working lives. Besides, at the same time this was going on, we had opportunity to get a sizeable partner from another country involved in this venture."

He stopped me. "What do you mean from another country?"

"We had some people from the Netherlands in this," I explained.

"How did you connect with these people from the Netherlands?" Judge Houk asked.

"The chairman of Amoco Oil Company, John Swearingen, and I have known one another for a long time," I replied. "John was doing business with these folks because Amoco wanted to explore in the Netherlands offshore. These people were good friends with the Queen and Prince, so they had a lot of discussion with Amoco as to how Amoco was going to work over there. Along the way, they mentioned they'd like to get involved in the oil and gas business in the United States. They asked if Mr. Swearingen knew someone he could refer them to, and John recommended Miller Brothers Oil Corporation in Michigan and suggested they might like to talk with us."

"Wait a minute," the judge said. "The chairman of Amoco told somebody from the Netherlands that you were good people and then these people call you up and you make a deal over the telephone?"

"At the time I had not yet met them; that is correct."

"Did you ever meet them?" the judge asked.

"Yes," I said, "I went on a drive pheasant shoot with them in England, where they have these large estates. Drivers go along with sticks whacking on the trees, and the pheasants keep running ahead and then all lift off. When they do, you have your assigned position where you stand and shoot." The judge was fascinated.

Back and forth it went like some zany exercise in stream-of-consciousness. Next he wanted to know other places I'd been, other things I'd done. I could see John Jones on the brink of convulsions, a huge smiled smeared across his face. It was evident the judge had taken a strong liking to me and that he was unabashedly intrigued to learn how a small company in Allegan, Michigan, was conducting a muscular business with key players on an international stage.

The judge circled back for more details about the hunt, and I explained how you'd be stationed in a place and have a person assisting you, a gulley, whose job was to work with two guns and pass you the loaded one to shoot.

"Once you've fired," I said, "you give your gulley the empty gun while he hands you the loaded one."

I also told him an anecdote that let him understand how, despite the international dealing and travel, we were still small-town boys in our DNA. At breakfast the day of the hunt, a man hurried over and sought to hand me what looked like a toothpick from the handful he was holding.

"No thanks," I said, "I'm fine." (My teeth felt clean enough.)

The guy clutching the handful smiled and said, "Take one of these picks; it designates where you stand in the hunt."

But what most conspicuously labeled me a novice was my clothing: way-way too new. In Europe, the measure of one's hunting experience is the age of his attire. The older, more threadbare and faded your togs, the more experienced you are at the driven pheasant hunt. So I had a whole lot to learn before I earned any aristocratic, hunting chevrons.

Much of this no doubt sounds trivial given the magnitude of our case, but it all was ostensibly important detail to Judge Houk as it sharpened his focus regarding who we were—and who we were not. For him it became clear, I'm convinced, that MBOC was not some faceless, mega-conglomerate engaged in a battle denominated in greed. His favorable ruling on our behalf underscored that we'd made a reasonable and compelling argument.

A final irony on the case bears a political note. (Or maybe I should say *apolitical*.) At the outset we knew the judge was a Democrat and wondered if he'd show some anti-

Republican bias as he adjudicated our case. In the end, there wasn't a whiff of that—no doubt due to the strength of our legal counsel (especially John Jones), the logic of our presentation, and the integrity of Judge Peter Houk, who has since retired from the bench.

On September 20, 1991, the trial concluded with monetary judgments totaling over $71 million ($46 million to Miller Brothers Oil Corp. and $25,475,000 to the private mineral owners). What ensued came as no surprise: the state of Michigan promptly appealed the verdict and the case was moved to the Court of Appeals, which would extend the legal process but not alter the outcome.

In February 1994, the Michigan Court of Appeals affirmed the 1989 Ingham Circuit Court decision that the drilling ban constituted a taking of property, but vacated the September, 1991, money judgments, remanding the case to the Court of Claims and Judge Houk for "further proceedings consistent with this opinion." That opinion states that while a taking did occur, it was temporary, and not permanent in nature, and that just compensation should have been based on fair rental value and not on fair market sale value of property taken. This ruling did not much affect the compensation due MBOC and its partners because more than ninety percent of the leases had expired, leaving the state liable for higher amounts in nearly all the lease holdings. MBOC and the state returned to the trial court to determine which leases had run-out and which were still valid, as required by the 1991 Court of Appeals ruling. Judge Houk reaffirmed the state's liability in the amount of $71 million. Additionally, in January 1995, Houk ruled the state should pay some of our attorney fees as well as interest on the principal of the judgments.

On September 25, 1995, Michigan Governor John Engler and Miller Brothers Oil Corporation signed an agreement that MBOC and their industry partners would receive compensation totaling $59.9 million. Designated deadline for payment: October 3, 1995.

But the Michigan House of Representatives procrastinated and failed to consummate debate and approval on time. Two later votes in October failed to garner the fifty-six votes needed for approval. Finally, a late session on November 9, 1995, saw the appropriation pass in the Michigan House by a 56-44 majority, then in the Senate, 22-13. On Monday, November 13, 1995, Governor Engler signed the settlement agreement; we signed on the 14th and received our check the same day. The twelve-year battle was over. We had won.

The Nordhouse Dunes Area case, in the end, came to serve as a gratifying win not just for MBOC, but also for everyone who puts on gloves to fight city hall when their cause is right. Sometimes justice does prevail—but I'll tell you, it always helps to have a tenacious little brother in the saddle beside you. A thunderous, posthumous thanks to Jack.

Gene and I were quick to give the preponderance of credit to Jack who had shepherded MBOC through our arduous ordeal. The Nordhouse Dunes verdict immediately became case law and has been used since in a number of other states as legal precedent. So ours was not a provincial victory—but a case with ramifications across the entire country. To this day, we field calls from industry lawyers and operators who seek to gather our background data and rationale so that they can mount a similar defense when a governmental agency seeks to take assets from them.

A special guest feature entitled *MICHIGAN CASE LOOMS LARGE: Miller Brothers Prevent "Takings,"* appeared in the May 30, 1997, edition of the Michigan Oil & Gas News. In the article William Perry Pendley, president and chief legal officer of the Mountain States Legal Foundation, referenced a battle in Wisconsin "waged between landowners who wish to make sensible, economic use of their property and a government entity that believes it has the right to 'Just say no!'" Only the names change... Pendley went on to summarize our case: "Thanks to the hard work, dedication and willingness to do whatever it takes by Miller Brothers, those landowners have reason to believe they will win and those who want to 'take' their property will lose and lose big.

"The U.S. Forest Service determined there were five acceptable drilling locations within the Nordhouse Dunes Area. In addition, the oil and gas lessees were willing to operate beyond the area's boundaries—from which directional drilling could be conducted. Nevertheless, the Michigan Department of Natural Resources ruled there were no circumstances under which hydrocarbons could be produced, and thereby prohibited their extraction. It was this decision that Miller Brothers took to court, asserting it violated the United States Constitution's Fifth Amendment ('nor shall private property be taken for public use without compensation'). Governments that hide their heads in the sand, pretending that land has no economic value, while prohibiting owners from making use of the land, MUST PAY A PRICE. That price is 'just compensation' due the landowners for unconstitutionally taking their private property.

"Today, millions of landowners throughout the United States are thankful for the remarkable tenacity and courage of the Miller Brothers in taking the Nordhouse Dunes case to court and emerging with a victory."

ANOTHER SHOT AT TELLING OUR STORY

Perhaps I made it sound like my resignation from the IPAA permanent presidency after the 1982 heart attack marked the end of my public advocacy for the oil and gas industry. Not by a long stretch.

Following is a segment of an address I presented to the Republican Platform Committee in Kansas City, Missouri April 13, 1992. (The President Bush referred to here is George Herbert Walker Bush.)

"The domestic petroleum producing industry in the United States is disintegrating before our very eyes, and the worst of this loss of a basic strength of America has occurred during the Bush administration. The impact of this on our economy and security is potentially disastrous.

"As one who voted for, supported and worked for the election of George Bush, I find it painful to say that his energy policy record is no record at all and is a great disappointment. I know that some loyalists to the president would respond to this by blaming the Democrats in Congress, and certainly Congress is due a large chunk of the blame. But our energy supply condition has deteriorated so far, so rapidly and so dangerously that the president should have addressed it long before now with an uncompromising effort."[19]

I continued for several pages with statistical support for my arguments as regards the decline of domestic petroleum exploration; the number of drilling rigs and people working then versus before; and empirical data pertaining to an increase in oil imports from thirty percent in 1982 to forty-three percent in 1992 while net oil prices dropped forty-three percent with a resulting twenty-one percent drop in gasoline retail pump prices.

In reality, retail pump prices are about the only statistic politicians, press, and public ever pay attention to—moaning, groaning and having fits if the price goes up a dime a gallon but gleefully chortling if the price drops a dollar, ignoring all impact upon the domestic producer and upon our natural energy security if other countries contrive to manipulate oil prices downward in order to weaken our abilities to mitigate our need for imports. Indeed, it may well have been foreign influence that helped swing the 2008 presidential election since it's obvious some parts of the world helped elect Mr. Obama, who had pledged a less get-tough strategy in the Middle East.

The old saw about "If I didn't have bad luck, I'd have no luck at all" is dead-center truth for the domestic independent oil and gas explorer/producer vis-à-vis our recent roster of U.S. presidents. It seems if we have one who understands business in general and the oil business in particular (as with both Presidents Bush), he tends to eschew tough decisions on energy policy lest a panic-mongering press accuse him of

---

[19] Appendix K – 1992 Republican Platform Committee Speech

cronyism. Conversely, if we have a president who doesn't understand business (which encompasses most Democratic high office holders, with the exception of the mediocre Jimmy Carter), then he's a member of that fraternity who have never signed the front of a paycheck. Either way it's tough for the oil industry—and for the nation's domestic energy security and growth—to hold a winning hand at the poker table of presidential politics.

Guess what happened in response to my lengthy, definitive proposals to the Republican Platform Committee. I was politely ignored. And the first President Bush subsequently lost the 1992 election to Democrat William J. Clinton, who seemed to latch onto my statement and use it as a manual to advocate just the opposite of every policy point I espoused. The second President George Bush was elected in the year 2000 and seemed to follow his dad's errant lead in energy policy matters.

Now, since 2008, we have a new president. America elected Democrat Barak Obama on his promise for change, and the revision he appears to be making is an attempt to eliminate the domestic oil industry altogether. Some of that derives from the misguided notation of what it means to be green, and the wild illogic of those who think sunshine, corncobs and wind are going to resolve all our energy woes. The rest of the irrationality seems driven by a socialistic desire to redistribute wealth with no litmus test of productivity. But as his defenders are saying at this writing, "He's new. He's been in office less than two years. Give him a chance." I hope we can afford that chance. So far it seems Rudy Giuliani's comment at the 2008 Republican Convention portends the sobering reality that: "Change is not a destination…any more than Hope is a strategy."

I can hear murmuring out there of "Oh John, that's so yesterday! So old school!" Well, folks, today we are importing approximately sixty-eight percent of the oil we use; we are greening ourselves into the poorhouse by allowing a strident press convince us that anything involved in making or producing things is inherently evil, while we export our jobs and money to other nations, some of which—under the guise of emerging economies—ignore all green and all human rights concerns.

Yesterday? Old School? You bet. Amen. But I assure you of this: if a future political party platform committee—and all of us—were to adopt and advocate the precepts conveyed in my 1992 statement, we still might have a fighting chance.

"Love not the world, neither the things that are in the world.
If any man loves the world, the love of the Father is not in him.
For all that is in the world, the lust of the flesh, and the lust of the eyes,
and the pride of life, is not of the Father, but is of the world.
And the world passeth away, and the lust thereof:
but he that doeth the will of God abideth forever."
(John 2:15-17)

REACHING TD

There comes a time when you reach TD (total depth), when you've drilled into the target zone and know whether or not you've done the job. Either you have a dry hole, or you have a producer. But you can drill no more. We seem to have reached TD here.

We lost brother Jack at a young 66 on January 14, 2000, and brother Gene is doing crushing battle with the physical and mental ravages of age, leaving me—the last Miller brother of the second generation—to tell our story. Reviewing this manuscript, I note too heavy use of the pronouns *I* and *me*. Even as narrator, it was not my intent to overwork those words, for it is truly *our* story: Reva's…Gene's…Jack's…and the broader Miller family's…*our* story.

Make no mistake: I remain passionate about our industry and love to talk about it, as my golf partners will readily attest, but age has banked my fires and I try not to get overly excited about the rash and treacherous course our nation is pursuing toward eternal dependence on foreign energy sources. I am constantly in contact with oil friends and associates as chairman of Miller Energy, Inc., although as president of the company, son Mike does the heavy lifting.

I could go on, but you have the essential drift of my life, which I would distill into a trio of themes. First and foremost, God has inordinately blessed the Miller clan within the contexts of both family and business, for which we are unspeakably grateful. Second, I hope any readers who are sensing self-doubt about their futures might screw tight their courage and find inspiration in my narrative to forge ahead with full-throttle faith. And finally, I pray my life exemplifies our need to unwrap the singular gifts God has entrusted us with, to hold loosely the stuff of this world, and to give back…and give back…and then give back some more.

God bless you, future generations.

CJM

"And I saw a new heaven and a new earth: for the first heaven and the first earth were passed away; and there was no more sea. And I, John, saw the holy city, New Jerusalem, coming down from God out of heaven, prepared as a bride adorned for her husband. And I heard a great voice out of heaven saying, Behold, the tabernacle of God is with men, and he will dwell with them, and they shall be his people, and God himself shall be with them, and be their God. And God shall wipe away all tears from their eyes; and there shall be no more death, neither sorrow, nor crying, neither shall there be any more pain: for the former things are passed away." (Revelation 21:1-4)

As the senior living past president of MOGA in terms of when I served, I met with 12 other past presidents in August, 2009 to nominate the 2010 MOGA Chairman Daniel Yohe. Left to right are: Gordon Wright (chairman, 1994–95), Byron Cook (president, 1980–81), Tom Mall (chairman, 2006–07), Bob Mannes (president,1982–83), Jack Harkins (chairman, 1990–91), Frank L. Mortl (President and CEO of MOGA) , Martin Lagina (chairman, 1996–97), Mike Miller (chairman, 2000–01), Jim Stark (chairman, 2004–05), me (president, 1966–67), Greg Fogle (chairman, 2002–03), Bill Myler (president, 1968–69), Bill Myler Jr. (chairman, 1998-99), and Dick Burgess (president, 1978–79).

APPENDIX A

MICHIGAN OIL AND GAS HISTORY

According to *A History of Michigan Oil and Gas Exploration and Production*, a catalogue published by the Michigan Oil & Gas Producers Education Foundation (MOGPEF) in connection with the Clarke Historical Library (in the Park Library at Central Michigan University's Mt. Pleasant campus) August 2005-February 2006 exhibit about the history of Michigan's oil and gas industry.

"Beginning in 1886, when C.A. Baily brought in three Dundee producers at about 550 to 575 feet near Port Huron, Michigan, each producing two or three barrels a day, there was a small amount of oil production in the Port Huron area. By 1910 the Port Huron Field had twenty-one wells producing less than 10 barrels a day each. The exact total production volume is not known. The Port Huron Field, located in Section 32-T6N-R17E, Port Huron Township, St. Clair County, was abandoned in 1921.

"In 1912 and 1913, a group of local capitalists and businessmen formed the Saginaw Valley Development Company to prospect for oil. During the group's second attempt, a hole near the geographical center of the city was treated with the downhole discharge of 100 quarts of nitroglycerine. The well "erupted with a spout of oil forty feet high from the mouth of the well and stood solid for four or five minutes." This spurt was followed a few minutes later by a second, higher column of oil that lasted about two minutes and also included natural gas.

"The discovery well, along with eight others nearby, did not pan out commercially. Ultimately the Saginaw Valley Development Company ceased operations, sold its equipment and the efforts 'determined without reasonable doubt that oil was a myth in this locality.' Fortunately there were those willing to try again.

"One person willing to look again was James C. Graves, a chemist by education, who worked for the Dow Chemical Company beginning in 1900. Graves closely followed the progress of Dow's brine wells. Graves left Dow to join the Saginaw Chemical Company. He was appointed president of the Saginaw Prospecting Company, formed in 1925 to revive the Saginaw area oil search. A test well was started July 25, 1925, on city-owned property known as Deindorfer Woods on the north side of Weiss Street.

"On August 29, 1925, the Saginaw News reported the well's success with a banner headline. The well produced an average of 23 barrels of oil per day for a few days, and averaged 17 barrels a day for the first 30 days."

The late 1920s through early 1950s proliferated with relatively shallow oil and gas field finds throughout the Lower Peninsula of Michigan.

The mid-1950s saw the discovery of the Albion-Scipio Trend, which has produced more than 125 million barrels of oil from a single reservoir, qualifying as a major oilfield by worldwide definition.

The late 1960s saw the discovery of the Niagaran Reef Trend, heralding the 1970s tripling of Michigan oil production and multiplying Michigan natural gas production six times.

The early 1980s discovery of deep strata natural gas production, still an emerging frontier, along with the potential of shallower zones and new technologies, signal even greater potential versus any of Michigan's previous petroleum history.

The late 1980s and early 1990s were punctuated by an unprecedented upsurge of drilling activity in the shallow Antrim Shale of Northern Michigan, which continues to be a major factor in Michigan natural gas production through refracturization and other advancing technologies.

The 1990s, with expanded Michigan market pipeline networks, saw Antrim Shale development increased and new horizontal drilling technologies ushered the state into a new era as a substantial natural gas production state. In the late 1990s, modern record low wellhead prices of oil and natural gas devastated the petroleum industry in Michigan and nationwide.

The early 2000s found Michigan petroleum explorers maintaining abbreviated drilling programs while recovering from the price devastations of the late 1990s. Drilling activity in Michigan has rebounded, with enhanced wellhead prices for oil and natural gas, averaging more than 475 holes per year 2000-2009.

APPENDIX B

THE C. JOHN AND REVA J. MILLER FAMILY

C. John Miller (1931) and Reva J. Pickitt (1931) – married 1951

Mike Miller (1954) and Pam (Morton) (married 1978)

> Amanda Miller (1981)
> Luke Miller (1982) and Paige Peterman (married 2010)
> Clinton Miller (1984) and Autumn Schweigert (married 2007)
> Jordan Miller (1986)

Cindy Miller (1956) and Craig Cunningham (married 2001)

> Drew Martin (1982) and Abby Benthem (married 2007)
> Dusty Martin (1985) and Alisha Maciejewski (married 2006)
> > Tucker Martin (2009)

Sara Miller (1958)

> Aimee Southwick (1982) and Peter Loeser (married 2006)
> Jonathan Southwick (1984) and Whitney Brennan (married 2006)
> > Kayla Southwick (2003)
> > Carter Southwick (2007)
> Grant Southwick (1987)
> Olivia Southwick (1989)
> Nathan Miller (1997)

Sally Miller (1960) and Bill Bufton (married 1982)

> Beau Bufton (1986)
> Brett Bufton (1987)
> Alexandra Bufton (1988)
> Ashlyn Bufton (1990)
> Alyson Bufton (1993)

APPENDIX C

THE ALBION-SCIPIO TREND

The Albion-Scipio Trend discovery put Michigan solidly in the ranks of oil and natural gas producing states. Again, according to MOGPEF/Clarke Historical Library's *A History of Michigan Oil and Gas Exploration and Production*:

"The story of the discovery well of Michigan's only 'giant' oil field, using the worldwide definition of having produced more than 100 million barrels of oil from a single contiguous reservoir is the stuff of dreams, and of oilfield legends.

"One version of the legend says that a fortuneteller told young Ferne Houseknecht that a 'black river of oil' lay beneath her property in Hillsdale County. Inspired by this revelation, Houseknecht enlisted Clifford Perry, a contract driller and sometimes farmer, to secure a drilling permit and drill a hole on her property. Another version of the story says that the Houseknechts were taking a cow to be bred, and on the way drove past a drilling rig where Perry was working and from their conversation a deal was struck. Whatever the truth the Houseknechts paid Perry to drill the Houseknecht 1 in Section 10 of Scipio Township, Hillsdale County.

"The well was begun in May of 1954. It took Perry more than two and a half years to drill the hole, often with months between periods of work.

"The well was drilled with no encouragement from the DNR or the petroleum industry." The late Ferne Houseknecht Bradford wrote, "The finances came from my family and friends."

"Persistence paid off when on January 7, 1957 at 4:00 p.m., oil was struck at 3,576 feet in the Trenton zone.

"The field would come to be known as the 'Golden Gulch' and would foster a 'boom' on a discovery-hungry petroleum industry to end a fifteen-year major discovery drought. The well triggered a drilling frenzy that would result in 734 wells producing more than 150 million barrels of oil and almost a quarter-trillion (225 billion) cubic feet of natural gas from a twenty-nine mile long by as much as a mile and a half wide underground "trench of porosity and permeability" angling southeast to northwest, spanning parts of Hillsdale, Jackson, Calhoun and nominally into Eaton counties.

"Although Ferne Houseknecht and her family paid for and benefited from the discovery well, some oil folk shared her suspicions about what lay underground in the area. Harold McClure Jr. and Detroit industrialist Max Fisher (Aurora Gasoline Company) had taken an enormous block of leases on acreage in the general area and drilled several test wells. Although they failed to make the discovery, McClure and Aurora were the first to offset the discovery well with a successful development well drilled in the 3,500 to 4,100 foot Trenton and Black River dolomite and were well positioned to benefit from the find.

"A little to the north, Mt. Pleasant's Tom Mask and K. P. Wood, along with attorney Ray Markel, put together a deal with McClure for a wildcat well near the City of Albion in Calhoun County. The test well, twelve miles northwest of the Perry-Houseknecht well, started to make oil from the Trenton in November of 1958, adding the "Albion" portion of the Trend's field name. Up in Pulaski Township, Mt. Pleasant's Turner Petroleum put the maraschino cherry on the Albion-Scipio sundae with a strong new well in Pulaski Township, Jackson County (about midway between the Scipio and Albion wells) and putting the Pulaski pearl in the Albion-Pulaski-Scipio Field necklace."

In truth, Cliff Perry was the quintessential oilman of his time: a promoter, producer, operator, and drilling contractor. I knew him well. During the two and a half years that Ferne's well was sporadically drilling, Cliff often visited our sites. Once when we were boring a well near Zeeland, Michigan, Cliff stopped by the rig to visit and I asked him how the Houseknecht #1 was doing.

"John," he said, "right now we're in the financial sand." Now I thought I had a broad working knowledge of Michigan geology, but I had never heard of the financial sand, so I asked him about it.

"The financial sand," he replied "is what we drill into once in awhile when I have to stop drilling until Ferne can come up with some more money. Then I go off and do other things until she says we can start up again. I don't think it's going to come out very good but I promised her I'd drill her well so I'll stick to it to the end." Cliff was a man true to his word…and that's how Michigan ended up with a discovery well in our biggest single reservoir field."

116

APPENDIX D

MICHIGAN OIL AND GAS ASSOCIATION (MOGA)

Prior to the founding of the present MOGA, a group of petroleum folk in the Muskegon area formed an organization in 1928 to establish higher crude oil prices. However, as the boom at Muskegon subsided and the Mt. Pleasant Field became the industry's focus, the Muskegon-based association faded away.

Overproduction causing slumping crude oil prices soon became a problem in the Central Michigan Fields. To deal with these problems, producers in Central Michigan, along with those from Muskegon and Saginaw, met in Mt. Pleasant and formed the Oil and Gas Producers Association in 1931.

That association was phased out when its leaders decided to reorganize with a broader member base and a better dues structure. This broader, better-financed organization was named the Michigan Oil And Gas Association. At a November 27, 1933 meeting, the newly formed MOGA elected Gordon Oil's Howard D. Atha as its first president. The organization continues to this day to represent the Michigan oil and natural gas exploration and production industry and supportive supply and service companies.

To date, there have been 41 Michigan oilmen elected to head MOGA as president until 1985 when the title was changed to chairman of the board and the title of president and CEO was bestowed upon the head of the MOGA permanent staff. 2010 would see the 42nd elected MOGA leader, Dan Yohe, sworn into office.

Seven individuals have served as the senior staff person of the Michigan Oil And Gas Association: Henry G. Hunt (1934-37); A. J. "Whitey" Weideman (1938-1941); W. B. "Wallie" Pardoe (1941-1945); Arthur H. Ledbetter (1947-1949); William Palmer (1949-1970); Frank L. Mortl (1971-present). Mortl, a General Motors management executive, joined MOGA in 1971 and has served the organization the longest, in a diligent, spectacular manner.

APPENDIX D (continued)

MOGA STATISTICS

MILLER FAMILY TENURES AS MOGA CHAIRMEN

Description	John 1966-1967	Gene* 1976-1977	Jack** 1988-1989	Mike 2000-2001
Drilling Permits Issued	835	1337	2040	N/A
Holes Drilled	824	1157	1581	1011
Oil Wells	125	256	103	21
Natural Gas Wells	38	127	836	660
Dry Holes	577	582	363	30
Facility Wells	-0-	99	-0-	-0-
Avg. Crude Price	$2.87/barrel	$12.00/barrel	$16.89/barrel	$25.61/barrel
Avg. Nat. Gas Price	$.58 - $.64 mcf	$.58 - $.79 mcf	$.58 - $.64/mcf	$3.66/mcf

*The Michigan Natural Resources Trust Fund was established during Gene's tenure as MOGA chairman.

**During Jack's tenure, the Michigan deep gas play was optimistically coming into its own as the learning curve ascendancy yielded fewer dry holes and the shallow Antrim gas play caused success rates to climb astronomically.

APPENDIX E
THE MICHIGAN NATURAL RESOURCES TRUST FUND

This trust fund serves six purposes:
- Protecting natural resources.
- Providing public access to Michigan waterways.
- Improving outdoor recreation in urban areas.
- Stimulating Michigan's economy through recreation-related tourism.
- Meeting community needs for outdoor recreation.
- Investing funds in projects that will yield the best long-term public recreation return.

As of December 2009, more than $735 million has been spent through the Trust Fund to support 1,267 projects in all 83 Michigan counties. Among the projects subsidized by the Michigan Natural Resources Trust Fund:
- Purchasing 70 miles of river frontage and more than 25,000 acres along two of the nation's top trout streams (the Au Sable and the Manistee).
- Helping the City of St. Joseph acquire 22 acres of Lake Michigan shoreline for Silver Beach County Park.
- Assisting Banks Township in Antrim County in obtaining more than 150 acres (including nearly a mile of frontage on Grand Traverse Bay).
- Obtaining 10,000 acres of undeveloped land in Mackinac County, including more than five miles of Lake Michigan frontage.
- Acquiring the tip of the Keweenaw Peninsula.
- Assisting in the acquisition for public use of Manistee County's CMS Arcadia/Green Point Dunes area as well as augmenting the City of Saugatuck's park system with acquisition of the precious Dennsion South property sand dunes.

In its early years, the fund also served as a means to help balance the state budget and subsidize the Michigan Economic Development Authority and other programs. Only small amounts of monies accrued to the fund's principal balance. Repeated raids over a period of seven years saw more than $100 million diverted to programs other than those in the original philosophy of the fund. Protests over raids on the fund grew louder and more widespread.

Voters in a statewide referendum election held in 1982 banned future raids on the fund. Although voters banned diversion of the fund for programs not related to its original intent by the state of Michigan, some critics continued to complain that tax rules made in the 1980s allowing oil and gas companies to deduct post-production costs from payments due the state unfairly diminished the amount of money paid into the Michigan Natural Resources Trust Fund.

APPENDIX F

1973 OIL PRICING AND POLITICAL CONTROLS

In Michigan, March of 1973 saw a crude oil price increase of twenty-five cents to $3.69 a barrel. It was our first price increase in two years. Average crude oil wellhead price in Michigan had hovered in a range between mid-$2.00 to almost-$3.00 per barrel since 1948 and now, for the first time, demand was pushing prices over the $3.00 mark. So things were lookin' up.

In the middle of June the same year, President Richard Nixon implemented wage and price controls, rolling back the twenty-five cent increase. By the end of 1973 the courts rescinded those constraints on EVERYTHING BUT CRUDE OIL prices, which would remain in effect, only to be adjusted multiple times in a complex system of price grades and become every accountant's nightmare, until January 20, 1981, when President Ronald Reagan removed them in one of his first acts in office.

By July 17, 1973, the Trans-Alaska Authorization Act, which cleared the way for the 800-mile pipeline, had passed the House of Representatives, but was deadlocked in the Senate—49 to 49. Vice-President Agnew, in his constitutional capacity as president of the Senate, cast the tie-breaking vote for the pipeline. Included in the bill was a provision to remove stripper oil from price controls while new oil (that discovered after the date of the bill) would be set at a level closer to, but still below, the world price. This was, of course, a resounding victory for domestic oil and gas explorer/producers as about eighty percent of America's production comes from stripper wells (those that produce less than ten barrels of crude per day).

APPENDIX G

PRESIDENT FORD'S PROPOSED LEGISLATION

In a special message to Congress on pending legislation July 26, 1975, President Ford wrote:

"In the weeks remaining in this session of the 94th Congress there is an opportunity to write a legislative record of which we can all be proud. Over the past 23 months I have sent legislative proposals to the Congress dealing with many vital areas of national concern. Some of these proposals have been enacted, some are nearing enactment, but many others have been stalled in the legislative process.

Today I am calling on the Congress to turn its full and undivided attention to this unfinished agenda of unfinished legislative business. If you do, the record you will take to the people will be a good one."

President Ford's list of urged legislation included:

NATURAL GAS DEREGULATION – This bill would be designed to reverse the declining natural gas supply trend as quickly as possible and to ensure increased supplies of natural gas at reasonable prices to the consumer. Under the proposal, wellhead price controls over new natural gas sold in interstate commerce would be removed. This action would enable interstate pipelines to compete for new onshore gas and will encourage drilling for gas onshore and in offshore areas.

ENERGY INDEPENDENCE AUTHORITY OF 1975 – This Act would establish a $100 billion Energy Independence Authority, a self-liquidating corporation designed to encourage the flow of capital and provide financial assistance, through loans and loan guarantees, to private enterprise engaged in the development of energy sources and supplies important to the attainment of energy independence but which would not otherwise be financed. This bill would also seek to expedite and facilitate the Federal regulatory and licensing process and to hasten the commercial operation of new energy technologies subsequent to the research and development phase.

NATURAL GAS EMERGENCY STANDBY ACT – This legislation would provide a limited exemption from the regulation of natural gas in interstate commerce. It would grant the Federal Power Commission authority to allow companies which transport natural gas in interstate commerce to meet the natural gas requirements of their high priority users by purchasing natural gas (a) from sources not in interstate commerce and (b) from other companies on an emergency basis free from the provisions of the Natural Gas Act, except for reporting requirements.

APPENDIX H

CITATIONS AND HONORS

"In grateful appreciation to C. John Miller, President of the Independent Petroleum Association of America, 1974-1975, for his forceful and articulate leadership, his basic integrity, his warm good humor, his penetrating insight and his boundless enthusiasm which harmonized the efforts of independent oil and natural gas operators in support of sound energy policies during a period of great uncertainty. He:

- inspired independents to become involved as never before in the politics and public affairs of our industry;

- instilled pride in the accomplishments of the domestic industry and its record of service to the consuming public and to the nation; and

- prompted greater understanding by the public and the political community of the competitive dynamics of the private enterprise systems as the best hope of solving the nation's energy problems."

ROGERS C. B. MORTON, SECRETARY OF THE INTERIOR

"Reposing confidence in the value of his advice and the soundness of his judgment as a representative of the petroleum industry, in the integrity and patriotism which have ensured him a distinguished place in the industry of which he is a part, I hereby designate and appoint C. John Miller a member of the National Petroleum Council."

1974 ALL AMERICAN WILDCATTER

"In recognition of his outstanding creative and courageous contributions to the petroleum industry in the search for the development of new oil and gas in the United States of America and to acknowledge his untiring efforts as a true wildcatter and champion of the free enterprise system, the All-American Wildcatter Committee designates C. John Miller as an All-American Wildcatter."

1975 HATS OFF AWARD

From the Texas Independent Producers and Royalty Owners Association (TIPRO): "Hats Off to C. John Miller...who has often been described as the petroleum industry's most effective spokesman today.

"John Miller has provided the kind of genuine leadership for independent producers perhaps unprecedented in our industry history. The times called for a great leader and he has certainly measured up. He not only provided insight into the complex issues bearing upon the well being of the independent, but also inspired others to rise to the great challenge. Himself an authentic independent oil and gas finder, he was able to speak out forthrightly as to industry realities in meeting the numerous political crises which could irreparably damage our nation and the free world at a critical juncture."

JOHN MILLER NIGHT – MOGA 1976

Fellow oilmen, family, employees, and industry related people gathered together for an evening in recognition of my state and national industry service. In a special supplement to the April 19, 1976, edition of the Michigan Oil & Gas News: "John is a successful businessman, which alone would earn him the 'quite a guy' label. In oil circles the tribute is given for his service as President of the Independent Petroleum Association from October, 1973, until October, 1975.

"That was a tough two-year period for the oil and gas industry and John quickly became recognized as the independent petroleum producer segment of the industry's foremost spokesman. In his 24 month IPAA presidential tenure, he appeared many times in front of Congressional Committees in Washington DC. During those months he logged an incredible 600,000 miles or more of travel to and from meetings with legislators, industry groups, and anyone who would pause a moment to hear the petroleum industry story. The 370 nights he spent away from home in those two years testify to the true sacrifice of this dedicated family man."

C. JOHN MILLER BUSINESS LEADERSHIP AWARD

In June 2000, Cornerstone University in Grand Rapids, MI inaugurated the C. John Miller Business Leadership Award to be given annually to those who have "demonstrated excellence, integrity, and significant achievement in business." I was honored as its first recipient.

HART PUBLICATION

In 2000, Hart Publications honored me as one of the *100 Most Influential People in the Petroleum Century*, a lineup including the venerable likes of Winston Churchill, Henry Ford, the founding fathers of OPEC, and two United States Presidents, George H. W. Bush and Ronald Reagan. What an accolade.

APPENDIX I

THE INDEPENDENT PETROLEUM ASSOCIATION OF AMERICA (IPAA)

"The Independent Petroleum Association of America (IPAA)[20] has represented independent oil and natural gas producers for three-quarters of a century. On June 10, 1929, President Herbert Hoover called a national and state conference to discuss and formulate a practical program for the conservation of America's natural petroleum resources. At that historic meeting at the Broadmoor Hotel in Colorado Springs, Colorado, oil operators, royalty owners, and land owners alike formed a new national association, the IPAA.

"Today, IPAA represents the thousands of independent oil and natural gas producers and service companies across the United States. Independent producers develop 90 percent of domestic oil and gas wells and produce 68 percent of domestic oil and 82 percent of domestic natural gas. A recent analysis has shown that independent producers are investing 150 percent of their domestic cash flow back into domestic oil and natural gas development—borrowing funds to enhance their already aggressive efforts to find and produce more energy.

"IPAA is a national trade association headquartered in Washington, D.C. It serves as an informed voice for the exploration and production segment of the industry, and advocates its members' views before the U.S. Congress, the Administration and federal agencies. IPAA provides economic and statistical information about the domestic exploration and production industry. IPAA also develops investment symposia and other opportunities for its members.

"Our Mission: The Independent Petroleum Association of America is dedicated to ensuring a strong, viable domestic oil and natural gas industry, recognizing that an adequate and secure supply of energy is essential to the national economy.

"Our Purpose: The Independent Petroleum Association of America is the national association representing the thousands of independent crude oil and natural gas explorers/producers in the United States. It also operates in close cooperation with 44 unaffiliated independent national, state and regional associations, which together represent thousands of royalty owners and the companies that provide services and supplies to the domestic industry."

---

[20] www.IPAA.org

APPENDIX J
CONGRESSIONAL TESTIMONY ON BEHALF OF IPAA

11-04-73	Senate Interior and Insular Affairs Committee
11-14-73	Committee on Interstate and Foreign Commerce (House of Representatives)
12-05-73	Special Subcommittee on Integrated Oil Operations (Senate)
01-23-74	Energy Subcommittee, Senate Finance Committee
02-01-74	Senate Committee on Interior and Insular Affairs
02-06-74	Ways and Means Committee (House of Representatives)
02-13-74	Finance Committee (Senate)
04-22-74	Commerce Committee (Senate)
06-06-74	Finance Committee (Senate)
07-12-74	Senate Committee on Interior and Insular Affairs
07-31-74	Senate Interior and Insular Affairs Committee
10-01-74	Committee of Interstate and Foreign Commerce (House of Representatives)
12-1974	Senate Commerce Comm. On Staff Working Paper of the Natural Gas Production and Conservation Act of 1975
02-20-75	Subcommittee on Energy and Power (House Interstate and Foreign Commerce Committee)
03-06-75	Committee on Ways and Means (House of Representatives)
03-07-75	Oil and Gas Production and Distribution Subcommittee (Senate Committee on Commerce)
03-17-75	Senate Finance Committee
05-19-75	Senate Interior and Insular Affairs Committee
07-16-75	Senate Finance Committee
07-22-75	House Ways and Means Committee
09-26-75	Energy and Power Subcommittee (House Interstate and Foreign Commerce Committee)
07-08-80	Republican Platform Committee Subcommittee on Energy: Cobo Hall (Detroit, Michigan)
04-13-92	Republican Platform Committee (Kansas City, MO)

APPENDIX K

(EDITED) REPUBLICAN PLATFORM COMMITTEE SPEECH 1992

"The domestic petroleum producing industry in the United States is disintegrating before our very eyes, and the worst of this loss of a basic strength of America has occurred during the Bush administration. The impact of this on our economy and security is potentially disastrous.

"It is no understatement to say that no problem of such importance has experienced such political neglect as our deteriorating energy supply and production capabilities. At some point, historians, as well as ordinary people, may well come to see an energy policy void of any sustainability as the single biggest failure of the Reagan-Bush Administrations. I frankly cannot imagine any Administration standing by dispassionately as witness to such economic collapse as has befallen our oil and natural gas exploration industry and the devastation of its total infrastructure since the mid-1980s.

"As one who voted for, supported and worked for the election of George Bush, I find it painful to say that his energy policy record is no record at all and is a great disappointment. I know that some loyalists to the President would respond to this by blaming the Democrats in Congress, and certainly Congress is due a large chunk of the blame. But our energy supply condition has deteriorated so far, so rapidly and so dangerously that the President should have addressed it long before now with an uncompromising effort.

"All polling on energy matters reveals that the American people do not understand the energy dilemma, or the implications of their growing dependence on foreign oil. Only the President, with his pulpit, can inform the people on this critical problem and seek their support and understanding in putting corrective actions in place. This the President should have done; instead, he has paid this grievous problem lip service, giving it a one- or two-sentence sound byte every six months or so.

"I cannot believe President Bush doesn't know or doesn't care, so I find his disinterest perplexing and disturbing.

"I express the disappointment reflected in the statement just made as a lifelong, involved Republican. I know the pundits and the cynics enjoy making light of platform promises by both national parties, but if platforms mean anything at all the country has a right to expect far more to protect its energy future than has been forthcoming from the current Administration in the past three and a half years. I would say that the Republican platform adopted in 1988 covered essential, common sense points on energy.

"On oil and gas policy specifically, I would like to excerpt stated goals from the 1988 platform and state the status of these glowing promises.

'We will adopt forceful initiatives to reverse the decline of our domestic oil production, if Republicans support:

- Repeal of the counterproductive windfall profits tax. <u>STATUS:</u> Yes.
- Maintenance of our schedule for filling the Strategic Petroleum Reserve to reach 750 million barrels by 1993 and encouragement of our allies to maintain similar reserves. <u>STATUS:</u> No.
- Incentives to save marginal wells, to encourage exploration for new oil, and improve the recovery of oil still in place. <u>STATUS:</u> No.
- Repeal of the transfer rule prohibiting independent producers from using certain tax provisions on acquired properties. <u>STATUS:</u> No.
- Elimination of 80 percent of intangible drilling costs as an alternative minimum tax preference items. <u>STATUS:</u> No.
- Exploration and development in promising areas, including federal lands and waters, particularly in the Arctic, in a manner that is protective of our environment and is best for the national interest. <u>STATUS:</u> No.

"I can assure you, in case you do not recognize the fact, that the unfulfilled promises listed here are the most meaningful ones.

"The windfall profits tax, which was unrelated to either windfall or profits, was repealed only after the collapse of oil prices made it imperative anyway.

"The repeal of the transfer rule in some cases enabled major oil companies to sell uneconomic properties to smaller independent producers who no longer sustain tax penalties from such transactions, but this does nothing to expand the nation's reserves which are in desperate need.

"In some cases, the Bush Administration has acted contrary to the actions pledged in the 1988 platform; for example, promising geologic basins offshore Northern California have been placed off limits to exploration by Presidential order until the year 2000. In no case has the President put his prestige on the line as an advocate of platform goals such as pushing for environmentally responsible exploration in infinitely small fraction of the Alaskan Wildlife Refuge.

"Neither has he pushed the U.S. Forest Service to stop its undeclared six-year moratorium on oil and gas leasing on millions of potentially productive geologic basins in the offshore western and southern United States.

"Among many needed actions now desperately called for, I would suggest the following:

1. First and foremost, the 1992 platform should declare that energy production and environmental protection are not mutually exclusive, and commit the next Republican administration to actions stimulating both greater energy productivity and effective protection of lands, forests, water, air and wildlife. Energy and the environment should be accorded equal status and commitment; our vital interest in both can and must be advanced simultaneously.

2. Oil and natural gas policies advocated in the 1988 platform should be updated and reaffirmed. Specific emphasis should be placed on:

    1.1 Elimination of tax disincentives for exploration and development embodied in the so-called Tax Reform Act of 1986. Inclusion of both intangible drilling costs (IDCs) and percentage depletion as "preference items" subject to the Alternative Minimum Tax (AMT) has put an effective cap on domestic drilling. Both depletion and IDCs should be eliminated as AMT preference items.

    1.2 Republicans should again commit to a policy in support of the principle of multiple-use public lands, including environmentally responsible oil and gas exploration in promising geological areas of the onshore Western United States, the Outer Continental Shelf and in the Arctic.

3. Republicans should be committed to streamlining of the licensing process for nuclear generating plants, and for advancing clean coal technology and use in fulfilling future demands for electric power in the United States. We have decommissioned three nuclear plants in the past three years and have licensed no new construction of generators since 1979; in the long-term interest of the nation, the nuclear option should be revived as quickly as practical.

4. Platform energy provisions should be buttressed by a firm directive to the President of the United States to elevate energy policy to prominence among the President's priorities, requiring that his personal attention be focused on the imperative need to reduce over-dependence on foreign oil. The platform should call upon the President to explain this pressing need in all its implications to the American people who will be critically affected by the failure, or the success, of public energy policy."

Thanks to God, who has made all things possible.

Thanks to my wife, Reva, for her lifetime of love and support.

Thanks to my family…for being them.

Thanks to the many business and personal friends we've made along the way
for their valued and continued good will.

Thanks to the Michigan Oil & Gas News magazine for the use of many of
the photographs contained herein.

C. JOHN MILLER is CEO of Miller Energy, Inc. of Kalamazoo, Michigan, and is the most honored senior statesman of the oil and gas independent oil and gas industry, having served as president of the Michigan Oil And Gas Association and as president of the Independent Petroleum Association of America. He is recipient of the Texas Independent Producers and Royalty Owners Association (TIPRO) *Hats Off* Award; Lone Star Steel's *Chief Roughneck Award*; the American Wildcatters Association's *Wildcatter of the Year Award*; and was selected by Hart Publications as one of the *100 Most Influential People in the Petroleum Century*. John and his wife, Reva, live in Marco Island, Florida.

JACK R. WESTBROOK is a Mt. Pleasant, Michigan, freelance writer, retired Managing Editor of the Michigan Oil & Gas News magazine and author of six previous historical photo review books, four for Arcadia Publishing Company: *MICHIGAN OIL & GAS; MT. PLEASANT* (Michigan) *THEN AND NOW; CENTRAL MICHIGAN UNIVERSITY*; and *ISABELLA COUNTY* (Michigan) *1859-2009*. He has also self-published a photo history of Isabella County, Michigan, one-room schools entitled *YESTERDAY'S SCHOOL KIDS OF ISABELLA COUNTY* and *THE BIG PICTURE BOOK OF MT. PLEASANT, MICHIGAN.*

www.ingramcontent.com/pod-product-compliance
Lightning Source LLC
Chambersburg PA
CBHW081131170526
45165CB00008B/2631